DEDICATION

This book is dedicated to my precious daughters, Laura and Leslie.

TABLE OF CONTENTS

Foreword
Purpose
1. Rainbow Girls — 1
2. The Miracle of Chuck, My Soulmate and our Life Together — 7
3. Hemingway — 38
4. I Died Last Night — 49
5. Light on the Rings — 60
6. Go to the Light — 64
7. Final Gifts — 82
8. My Journey with Chronic Pain — 84
9. GI Bleed — 102
10. Australia — 104
11. The Merkabah — 107
12. My Grandchildren's Quilts — 109
13. P.E.O. — 114
14. Sydney's Wings — 116
15. Riley Crossing — 118
16. Prayer Flags — 123
17. Lessons from Denece — 126
18. Godsends in my Life — 129
19. How I Choose to Live My Life — 134
20. Acknowledgements — 136
21. About the Author — 138

FOREWORD

I met Denece Praeger in 1997. She was warm, open, and there was something special about her that I couldn't articulate for a while. I was struck by how she viewed life, how she made room for everybody.

Denece brings out the best in me. Her effect on me is solidly profound. When I am with her, I feel peace, calm, and like I am standing on solid ground with her.

Never have I met anyone like her before or since and I don't imagine I will.

Come, meet this extraordinary woman and her amazing experiences coming out of who she is, what she values, and how she sees life. To experience who she is, you'll have to meet her through these pages.

    Enjoy the ride!!!

    Diana Yost, LPC

PURPOSE OF THIS BOOK

All around us, there are miracles in our lives. We just need to open our eyes and hearts to recognize them and give thanks to God for walking this life with us.

This prayer sits in front of me in my office: "Turn it over to God and let go."

Good morning, this is God
Today I will be handling all of your problems.
Please remember that I do not need your help.

If the devil happens to deliver a situation that you cannot handle,
do not attempt to resolve it. Kindly put it
in the SFGTD (Something for God to do) box.
It will be addressed in MY TIME, not yours.

Once the matter is placed into the box, do not hold onto it nor remove it.
Holding on or removal will delay the resolution of your problem.
If it is a situation, you think you are capable of handling,
please consult me in prayer to be sure that it is the proper resolution.
Because I do not sleep, nor do I slumber,
there is no need for you to lose sleep.
Please rest my child.

If you need to contact me, I am only a prayer away.
My prayer line is open twenty-four hours of your day.
I love you and will always be with you wherever you may go.
As with all good things, pass my message on.

Love, GOD

My top ways to listen and watch for miracles:

•Inner voice

My inner voice is GOD talking to me. I try to listen carefully but sometimes I don't listen, like writing this book. GOD has been telling me to write this book for seven years. I kept saying back, "I'm not a writer" or "I only have one year of college. How can you think I could write a book?"

•Intuition

Many times in my life I have just "known" that I was to do something. Intuition is something I listen to.

•Happenstance

When something just "happens", I recognize it and call it a miracle.

•Unbelievable

We might say to ourselves, "That is just unbelievable" when it is a miracle.

•Blessing

When you have been blessed by a person coming into your life – grandchild, soulmate, or a Godsend, recognize these are miracles in your life.

•Coincidence

Finding the two letters that Chuck wrote me while I have been writing this Book – coincidence or miracle? I choose to look at them as miracles.

•Gem

Bonnie Smith, my beta reader, and now looks and finds the "gems" in her life. My purpose for this book is to share with you, the reader, the miracles that have happened in my life. Hopefully it will help you to recognize that miracles are also happening in your life.

As G.K. Chesterton wrote, "The most astonishing thing about miracles is that they happen."

RAINBOW GIRLS

Growing up, we did not have a church home. Daddy was raised Baptist and Mother was raised Methodist. They both had a falling out with their churches, so we never joined a church with Sunday School, Bible Study, etc.

I felt left out when my friends talked about their church and the church activities. I was looking to belong to an organization that could teach me and mold me to be the best person I could be. Then I found those possibilities in Rainbow Girls.

The International Order of the Rainbow for Girls is a Masonic youth service organization that teaches leadership training through community service. Young women learn about the value of charity and service through their work and involvement with their annual local and Grand (state or county) service projects.

The Pathway of Initiation

"I do set my bow in the cloud, and it shall be for a token of a covenant between me and the earth. (Genesis 9:13 KJV)

What is the International Order of the Rainbow for Girls?

The quest of girlhood on the journey of life

A hidden gate between reality and enchantment

An ideal made real by enchantment

What does Rainbow Teach?

A belief in the existence of a Supreme Being

The great truths of the Holy Bible

To seek dignity of character

A conception of higher things in life

Effective leadership

Church membership

Patriotism

Co-operation with equals

Love of Home

Service

Mother and Daddy were both involved in the Free Masons. Daddy was a thirty- second-degree Mason and Mother was active in Eastern Star. For a daughter of Mason, the Rainbow Girls program is available. The boys have DeMolays.

When I was in seventh grade my friend Barbara Ferguson Gillium invited me to join Rainbow Girls. Barbara told me about the Christian works that Rainbow Girls did, so I was excited.

After Barbara and I talked, I came home from school and found my dad working in his wood shop in the garage. He and his father made furniture for our home. Most of these pieces are still in the family today. I walked in and interrupted Daddy. "Do you know about Rainbow Girls, and can I join the organization?"

Daddy started crying, because he had been waiting a long time for one of us to be interested in Rainbow Girls. Susan, Beverly, and I all joined at the same time. I fell in love with the organization, because I had finally found my church home.

Our Chapter, "San Antonio Assembly Number Three, Order of the Rainbow Girls," met in the Masonic Hall in downtown San Antonio. The Chapter was made up of girls from all over San Antonio. We went to dances with the DeMolays, the boy's organization from Free Mason's.

From seventh grade to my junior year in high school, I started going through all the Chairs:

Charity: teaches about charitable deeds.

Hope: teaches that hope is always there for us.

Faith: teaches that faith is our constant companion. She is the officer who guides new candidates throughout an initiation ceremony.

Recorder: records minutes and handles correspondence.

Chaplain: leads in prayers.

Drill Leader: leads the officers in their floor work and leads guests around the Assembly Room.

Worthy Associate Advisor: duties like a Vice President. Presides over a meeting in the absence of the Worthy Advisor.

Worthy Advisor: presides at meetings and plans activities for her term like a President. It is the highest office of an Assembly.

There are Seven Bow Stations that teach lessons about the colors of the rainbow and their corresponding virtues.

Love (Red): in all its forms.

Religion (Orange): the importance of religion in all its forms (based on love and forgiveness).

Nature (Yellow): its importance in daily life.

Immortality (Green): the understanding that death is a part of life.

Fidelity (Blue): emphasis on being honest and dependable.

Patriotism (Indigo): encouraging citizenship to our country.

Service (Violet): service to others which binds all the colors together.

When you are the Worthy Advisor, you serve for four months. You pick your theme, symbol, and project for the Chapter to work on. You have a reception for the Chapter and their families. My whole family helped with my reception. Mother made my formal gown, just like she made all my clothes.

My theme was "Our Place Before the Altar."

My colors were pink, white, and gold.

My flowers were pink and white carnations

My symbol was an altar with the open Bible on it.

My Speech Before the Chapter

Below is the speech I wrote and delivered in my junior year of high school to the entire assembly when I accepted the position of Worthy Advisor:

"Each Installation, a new corps of officers stands before the altar to accept the responsibilities of their office. Each time I was among the corps of officers the experience caused me to become aware of its significance. Thinking about it diligently, I have come to realize that I wanted to understand the meaning of "Our Place Before the Altar."

"So many opinions have been formed, yet so few people know, or even try to find out, the true meaning of the altar. In everything we do or say, we know God is watching over us and we can trust in Him.

"An altar can be made of many types of material and can appear in many different ways. It can be a rock in the woods, a mecca in Egypt, or an animal. It does not need to be in a church. Just as we can pray anywhere, an altar can be present anywhere.

"The altar is the center of all Rainbow activities. Lying on our altar is a Bible which represents the principal light in the Rainbow. When one kneels before the altar, one dedicates herself to a life of active service and teaching others the true lessons of the Rainbow.

"The reason I chose "Our Place Before the Altar," was to strengthen and renew my faith in God and our fellow man. For it is at the altar that a girl learns what it is to grasp firmly the hand of God. The Bible teaches this kind of father. No girl is ever alone.

"But a Rainbow girl learns and knows that no one on this earth will ever walk alone. The altar is never too crowded nor the sight of God too limited not to be aware of every person on this earth, at any time. As Rainbow girls,

occupying a place at this altar, it is our place to enlighten others so they may realize that they too occupy a place at this altar.

"The altar represents the one true supreme being, which is expressed by the guiding scripture in Matthew 23: 20-22.

"'Who so, therefore, shall swear by the altar, sweareth by it, and by all things thereon.' (Matthew 23:20 KIV)

"'And whoso shall swear by the temple, sweareth by it, and by him that dwelleth therein.' (Matthew 23:21 KIV).

"'And he that shall swear by heaven, sweareth by the throne of God, and by him that sitteth thereon.'" (Matthew 23:22 KIV)

As I reread this speech to share in my book, I was amazed and proud of what I wrote. I created three scrapbooks of my time growing up, from birth to graduation. I am amazed that I kept this speech in my scrapbook, and it was actually good. The Rainbow Girls organization and my part in it helped me to become who I am today. Finding the speech was a miracle.

On the day when I took office, my officers presented me with this poem, a gift from the Chapter:

"From love to service these years have led,

From morn till night

Even as you lie in bed.

Dear Denece, a friend so true,

You have our blessings always.

God bless you."

From the Bible of Rainbow Girls: *"Mankind's place in life is always to follow God's footsteps as best as we can. Often, we get tired of trying to find that not-so-worn path and decide to find a path of our own, defying God's will. In times like those when we must humble ourselves and ask for forgiveness from our eternal Father, our place is surely before the altar."*

When Chuck and I got married and had our daughters, I wanted them to experience Rainbow Girls. But we did not have a Chapter close to us. It would have been at least an hour from our home. However, we did find a church home in the Methodist church, and we taught our girls about God, encouraging them to find their own path.

MIRACLES

The Miracle here was finding an organization that taught me service for others, leadership, and to solidify my faith in our Lord. Thank you to Barbara Ferguson for giving me the gift of the Rainbow.

The Rainbow also gave me a purpose for writing this book, to tap into my emotions. Hopefully, this book will help others to tap into their emotions.

The Miracle of finding my speech after sixty years, forgetting that I even kept it in my scrapbook.

THE MIRACLE OF CHUCK, MY SOULMATE, AND OUR LIFE TOGETHER

Throughout my marriage to Chuck, many miracles happened.

I was raised in a military family. We did not have a lot of money. Daddy was enlisted with the Army stationed in San Antonio and worked at the Fort Sam Houston base. Mother worked at night as a pediatric night nurse. She went to work at 10:30 p.m. and came home at 7:00 a.m. After dinner, while we cleaned up from supper, she made clothes for all three of us.

I remember when Susan got a new dress and I thought, *I can't wait until she outgrows it. Then after Beverly gets it, I finally get it.*

Mother loved for us to play with her hair, so I would brush her hair while she made our clothes. Mother made the meals, and the three of us did the dishes. We had no dishwasher. We had a washing machine and no dryer, so we hung the clothes on a line in the back yard. Living in San Antonio, Texas, I vividly remember running on the scorching hot grass to hang the clothes up, then running again to take them down.

After I got married, I asked Mother, "Why didn't we have a dishwasher or a dryer for our clothes?"

She said, "Why would I need those when I had three girls that could do the dishes and hang up the clothes?"

Chuck was from a professional family. His dad, Charlie, was a vice president of Mosher Steel Company and his mother, Mary V. was a stay-at-home housewife. Chuck's sister, Barbara, was five years older. When Barbara went off to college, and Chuck's dad traveled, he and his mother would "create" in the kitchen, making amazing dinner meals. They made a huge mess but "Juanita" their maid, cleaned it up.

Chuck's dad traveled all the time from coast to coast. Chuck's mom and dad had a dynamic marriage. They would fight with each other, then be passionate. One of the first times I met Chuck's parents, we were sitting in the dining room having dinner.

Mom and Dad were arguing, Mom got so mad, she stood up and threw her glass of bourbon into Dad's face. I was so upset, I left the table, went into the bathroom and threw up.

When Chuck came in to see if I was okay, all I could say was, "They're going to get a divorce."

"No," Chuck said, "They do this all the time. They have great conversation and then openly argue with each other."

From Charlie and Mary V., I learned how to have a great marriage. They had passion, kindness, respect, and they argued, but still showed great love for each other.

Everything in my family was at an even keel. I never saw my parents fight or be romantic with each other — ever.

Chuck and I met on a blind date August 11th, 1966, arranged by Kirke Jefferies and Janene Council. Kirke was Chuck's best friend in junior high school. Janene was with me in high school and in Rainbow Girls. They arranged the date as a joke because we were as different as night and day, and they thought we would never get along. They wanted to laugh as they watched us spar.

On our first date, Chuck came to the door in a Hart Schaffner Marx suit with a gold vest, wing-tip shoes, and a pipe. The company of Hart Schaffner Marx suits was founded in Chicago in the late 1800s with a long history of innovation that revolutionized men's suits.

I answered the door in a navy linen dress my mother had made. It had peplum sleeves and large Hawaiian flowers. I wore orange flats, orange papier-mâché earrings and topped it off with an orange papier- mâché bracelet. Papier-mâché consists of paper pieces or pulp, sometimes reinforced with textiles, bound with an adhesive, such as glue, starch, or wallpaper paste. In the sixties it was the rage.

From our initial meeting we were both smitten. We saw stars, our hearts fluttered, and we both knew we had met our soulmate.

Chuck was a pre-law student in high school. He debated in tournaments all over Texas and Louisiana. In college at The University of Texas in Austin, he majored in law and history. His plan was to be a lawyer when he graduated.

I was going off to my first year of college at Sam Houston State Teacher's College in Huntsville, Texas. My plan was to be a speech pathologist.

Kirke, Janene, Chuck, and I went to see the movie *What Did You Do in the War, Daddy?* I laughed all the way through the movie. Chuck sat beside me and pointed out, "That's wrong, that's wrong, that's wrong," from a historical standpoint.

After the movie we went back to Chuck's apartment that he was renting for the summer. He took math during the summer session at San Antonio Community College. He had put a blueberry pie in the oven and forgot to take it out before he left for the movie. When we entered his apartment, we realized the pie had burned.

I had just turned eighteen and Chuck was twenty-one. I would *never* have gone to a man's apartment, but I felt safe since Kirke and Janene were with us.

We danced to music and had a wonderful time. I decided to go to the bathroom, and I took off my earrings. I wanted Chuck to call me for another date, so I left my earrings in his shirt pocket. Chuck had no clue I had done this until later when he found my earrings. He did call to ask me out on another date.

When my parents met Chuck for the first time, they both fell in love with him. Chuck and my mother would have coffee together and just talk. Mother told me, "If you don't marry him, I will."

When I was in high school, I would date a boy for three weeks, then break up or the boy would break up with me. Mother said, "When you date someone longer than three weeks, that's who you'll marry." She was right. We dated for one year and one week, and then we married.

My dad loved Chuck. They would talk, work with their hands, smoke cigarettes and drink together at the house.

Chuck and I dated for three weeks before I left for college. Two days before I would leave, Daddy and Chuck decided I needed to get drunk in a safe environment so I would know what it felt like to get drunk. Mother was at work.

Daddy and Chuck gave me rum and Tab™. As the night progressed, I got very drunk. The room spun and I could not walk straight. They opened the pullout couch in the family room. Chuck sat in a chair next to the couch to make sure I was safe and wouldn't hurt myself. He was sweating bullets because he knew my mom was going to be mad and disappointed in him for letting this happen. He was right.

When Mother came in from work and saw me, she was pissed that Daddy and Chuck had gotten me drunk. I finally fell asleep, and Chuck went back to his apartment with his tail between his legs.

I will say that their tactic of getting me drunk worked, because I never drank in college. I've also never had rum and Tab™ again. The memory is still vivid in my brain.

When I left for college, Daddy and Chuck took me to Sam Houston State Teacher's College in Huntsville, Texas and helped me get settled in my dorm room. Chuck went back with Daddy, then closed his apartment. He went back to Austin to finish his senior year.

Chuck and I dated long distance, seeing each other every weekend for a year. He would pick me up, and we would go to Houston to be with his parents.

Even though I did not drink or smoke, by the end of my freshman year, I learned every curse word in the book. I thought I was a real grownup. My parents never cursed. The only curse word my mother would use was "shit," and she said it so fast you had to really listen to understand what she was saying.

After dating for five months, Chuck proposed. We were at the Barn Door in San Antonio at Christmas. As he proposed he said, "There is just one thing I need for you to do before we can be married. I need for you to clean up your potty mouth."

I thought about which words I would give up. I finally looked at him and said, "I'll give up everything except 'shit.'"

Chuck was happy with that, so we were officially engaged. We were both over the moon with happiness. All I had to do was complete my freshman year and Chuck his senior year.

Chuck was a prolific writer. He wrote to me at least twice a week. I kept all his letters but did not keep mine. Before I started creating this book, I put all of Chuck's letters in three 12x12 albums.

As I was writing this book, I walked into my sewing room and there on my cutting table, I found this letter in the center of the table all by itself. I thought I had put all of the letters in the albums.

Dear Denece,

Do I feel good! I went outside and ran really hard. I thought I was going to collapse. Then I came in, yanked off my clothes, and turned the hot water on in the bath. I proceeded to sit in there with the door closed. I sweated two gallons. Then I took a hot shower and tapered it off with cold water. I felt like a million bucks. Darling, if I could or would do that every night, I would literally have no problems, never be tired, and would sleep soundly every night.

Well, my love, it's 2:30 a.m. I'm still not asleep. I just can't go to sleep. How I wish you were by my side!

Denece, here is an important point for you to consider. If I do go in as an enlisted man, you my dear, will have to be making good money for us to get married. The only type of job you can get, that will pay the kind of money we will need, is secretarial. As of now you are flunking shorthand and doing poorly in typing. This really worries me, darling, for you have to be qualified. I wish I did not have to ask you to work but since we both want to get married, there is no other way.

Darling, I don't want to make you mad. I just need to point out something to you. When you go to the employment service, they will ask you how fast you can type. There will be girls who can type seventy, eighty, and ninety words a minute. The question you should ask yourself is, "Can I beat them?"

I have more questions I want you to sit down and think about and I have one favor, don't get excited and don't make excuses. Judge by your previous performance, okay?

Have I studied and learned the techniques for me to get a job and do well in that job?

Am I willing to sacrifice the things I really want and to do things I really hate but know what will make my dreams come true?

Do I want marriage so badly that I will work my head off doing the things I hate? At school have I proven this? Have I proven myself ready to take on real responsibility?

Darling, you see these questions pop into my mind about you, just as these questions should pop into your head about me. You see, darling, you are the turning point or focal point as to marriage. If you see failures in your answers to my questions, then start making up for them. Stop talking to everyone and deprive yourself of pleasurable moments of fun and sleep during the weekday. Get the idea out of your mind that it is too late. It's never too late for hard work.

Sweetheart, I am placing you on the spot. You are going to have to get a job on your own and by your ability, which will be seen in time. I will judge yours and my chances of making it in the near future.

Do I seem hard and unfair? After you read the letter for the third time, ask that question again. Judge yourself, honey, and make it hard on yourself. That way you can see what lies ahead of you more realistically. If you make it easy on yourself, you will only end up a failure.

Denece, I say all of this for yours and my sake. I love you, darling, more than anything else and it is only because of that fact that I write the later part of this letter. We have a hard road ahead of us. It's a road you know nothing about. And for that reason, I hope to scare you a little and make you really start worrying. That is the first step to success, my love.

Well, I am going to close. Please don't be mad, Denece. I love you. Some of the questions I have asked are the questions every young maturing individual must ask and answer in the affirmative. I ask myself questions like that every day. Most of the time, my answers scare me. You see, we are all in the same boat. What we have to do is learn from our answers and failures and then try to catch up. It seems I have been trying to catch up all my life. And in most instances, I have succeeded.

Darling, I love you and wish you good night.
Love, your devoted husband.

Hundreds of women might have been angry with the letter. I was not because it helped me put in perspective my part in our getting married. I changed my major from speech pathology to business. I changed my course structure and started taking typing and dictation so I could go out into the world and help make money for us to start our lives.

While we were in school, Chuck offered me a book that he treasured. It was *The Prophet* by Kahlil Gibran. Gibran was born in 1883 and died in 1931. He was a poet, philosopher, and artist, born in Lebanon, a land that produced many prophets. He made his home in the United States during the last twenty years of his life. He also began to write in English. *The Prophet* and his other books of poetry, illustrated with his mystical drawings, are known, and loved by innumerable Americans who find in them an expression of the deepest impulses of man's heart and mind. He talked about the two pillars separately holding up the house. Chuck would be the bread winner, and I would be a stay-at-home mom.

I started reading it and fell in love with the book. In one of the first chapters, he talks about marriage. He is talking about one house and that it takes two pillars to hold up the house, Chuck on one end and me on the other. Both of our beliefs and lives build a house together. We do not come into this marriage for us to meld together into one person. But both of us held up our end of the house. We patterned our marriage after the lessons we learned from the book.

There is a chapter in the book about children. Two beings come together to make a child. The child does come from you but then after the child is born, the child becomes its own person. Chuck and I raised our girls by honoring and encouraging their strengths and hoping to guide them through their challenges. But in the end, it was their life and their path to walk.

After I read the book, I returned it to Chuck. I had marked in pencil the passages that hit home to me. He got mad at me, because I marked in his book. He never marked in any of his books. He did forgive me, but I also never wrote in any of his books again.

When Chuck graduated from The University of Texas, he moved to San Antonio and set himself up in an apartment that once was a hotel. He had one bedroom, bath, kitchen and living room combined.

He started his first job with the Mosher Steel Company in San Antonio. They had a mill, and his job was to scrub out the vats that housed the liquid steel. He had to strip at the door, so he did not bring the shavings from the mill into his apartment.

My older sister, Susan, got married in June of 1967. Chuck was a groomsman at her wedding. After the wedding Chuck went back to Houston with his parents for a few days. When he got home, he received a letter saying it was time for him to take his physical for the draft. This was the Vietnam War era.

He called to tell me, and I started crying. We had planned to get married. But now we were getting married before he went to basic training.

Sobbing, I came out of the bedroom. I told my mother the situation and the dates we were looking at for the wedding. Could they do a wedding for me just two months after Susan's wedding?

My sweet mother said, "We'll go pick out your dress on Thursday."

We started planning our wedding for August 19, 1967. What did the world look like at that time?

- The president of the country was Lyndon B. Johnson and vice president was Hubert Humphrey.
- Thurgood Marshal was the first Black judge appointed to the Supreme Court.
- The Vietnam War was escalating.
- The 25th Amendment to the Constitution fixed the Line of Succession — a first for our leaders.
- Gas was thirty-three cents a gallon.
- The median family income was $7,933 and the median price for a home cost $22,700.
- A new car costs $3,212 dollars, and minimum wage was $1.40 an hour.
- Postage stamps cost five cents, and bread cost 25 cents.
- The United States population had reached 200 million.

Chuck and his dad were trying to get him into the reserves. Three days before our wedding, his dad called and said, "Chuck, you have to come to Houston to get signed into a reserve unit in Baytown, Texas."

Chuck told my mom, "Sue, I promise I will get Denece back to San Antonio in time for our wedding." So off we went to Houston, then Baytown for Chuck to sign up for the reserves.

Before the wedding, Chuck, his mother, and I went to pick out my wedding ring. We had no money, so we bought a simple wide gold band which is what I wanted. In front of his mother, Chuck told me, "On our 25th wedding anniversary, you can pick out the diamonds of your choice."

I never took my band off. Three years into our marriage, I looked at the inscription Chuck had engraved on the inside of the ring. It read "Love for all eternity."

On our 25th wedding anniversary, we went to the jeweler to pick out my diamonds. I chose five marquise diamonds in graduating sizes. One diamond for each of our five years.

The jeweler asked, "How important is the engraving?"

I looked at Chuck with my eyes wide and he said, "Very important. Don't touch the engraving."

Our wedding went off without a hitch. While I was getting dressed Chuck's mother came up to me, took both my hands in hers, and said, "Honey, I did the best I could. He's all yours now."

My mother went to Chuck and said, "We can cancel this right now and let Denece finish her college education."

Chuck looked at her and said, "Sue, she's all mine now."

We were married on August 19, 1967. As Chuck and I were driving back to San Antonio from our honeymoon, we were driving down Garrity Road in Terrell Hills, getting ready to turn on to Lilac Lane, I said to Chuck, "Oh my gosh! They know what we've been doing." In my innocence, I did not know how to face my parents.

When we went into the family home, we packed up my clothes and my three albums of Barbara Streisand. That was all I brought to begin our life together.

Chuck packed up his apartment with books and his classical music. His record albums took up the entire backseat. He loved Bach and Vivaldi the most.

We also had our wedding gifts. We had not registered china or silver because Chuck's Mom and Dad told us we would inherent theirs on our 25th wedding anniversary. Mom and Dad were still entertaining and using their china and silver. Because we had no dishes, my parents gave us a full set, 12-place setting of my paternal grandmother's Depression glass. Mother and Daddy also gave us a full set of Cutco knives. I still use those knives to this day.

We packed Chuck's car, a 1965 White Plymouth, named Athena. He named her Athena because he loved Greek mythology. We had our albums, my clothes, and in the trunk, our wedding gifts. The car was full.

We started our lives in Houston, living with Chuck's Mom and Dad until we could get jobs and a place to live. Chuck got an interview with the Armco Steel Company. I went to Snelling and Snelling to interview for job placement.

Chuck dropped me off at Snelling and Snelling. He then left for the Armco Steel interview. "Wait here. I'll pick you up when my interview is over." He told me the interview was in Richmond. I had never lived in Houston, so I had no idea if he meant Richmond Avenue or Richmond, Texas.

My interview with Snelling and Snelling only took an hour. The letter that Chuck sent me in college turned out to be so correct. When I changed my studies to secretarial, it made all the difference in my ability to get a job.

When I finished my interview with Snelling and Snelling, I stood in front of Battlestein's department store. I had no money on me and cell phones were not invented yet. The only way I could call Chuck's mom was to go into the department store and use their phone.

After three hours of waiting, I called Chuck's mom to ask her to please come and pick me up. She told me, "I always taught my kids to stay where I let them off. Just stay there, I'm sure Chuck will be back."

So I went out front to the same display case I had been standing in front of. At least while Battlestein's was still open, I had a place to go to the bathroom, and it also had air conditioning. After 5:00 the store closed.

A police officer (one of my first God-sends) was directing traffic in front of the store. After the traffic slowed down, he came over to me and said, "Young lady, why have you been standing out here all this time?"

"I'm waiting on my husband to come and pick me up."

"How long have you been standing out here?"

"Five hours."

The police officer said, "Come with me, young lady." He took me to the pharmacy that was in direct sight of the department store. He called Chuck's mom and said, "This is officer such and such. You need to come and pick up this young lady. It is going to get dark soon, and she has no business being in downtown Houston after 5:00."

We went back to Battlestein's, and he stood with me until Chuck's dad arrived. At the same time, Chuck pulled up. After I got in our car, Chuck went to talk to his dad. Dad was livid because he had just come home from downtown Houston, then had to turn around and go back.

When Chuck got back in the car he said, "You think you're mad. You should see Dad!"

I was furious but then Chuck explained that the interview lasted five hours and had gone very well. He also apologized that he had no way to contact me.

"Well, you're never going to go to work for that company," I said, still mad.

But Chuck did work for Armco Steel. I got a job at an architectural firm as a secretary. I was very glad I had listened to what Chuck said in the letter about changing my major.

We moved into our first apartment, two bedrooms, one bath, kitchen and living room. I got pregnant with our first child while I was on birth control. We had only been married for three weeks so we were both shocked that I was pregnant, but still so excited.

During Christmas of 1967, Chuck received a letter stating that he would be relocating to El Paso, Texas to begin his training for the reserves. He was going to Boot Camp. We put our stuff in storage, and I moved in with Chuck's mom and dad.

After Boot Camp, Chuck went to Fort Huachuca, Arizona for advanced training. He would be there for three months. He became the head cook for his unit.

Chuck and I missed each other terribly. We decided I would quit my job and move to Phoenix to live with his older sister, Barbara, and her husband Stu.

I slept in their youngest son's room. I would wake up each morning to our nephew Corey's beautiful brown eyes smiling at me.

I lived with Barbara and Stu for three months. Chuck and I thought we would see each other often but it only happened once. When we moved back to Houston, Chuck continued to serve his six years of reserves, going to Kentucky for one weekend each month. While he was in the reserves, Chuck went back to Armco Steel, and I stayed home to prepare for our first child to be born.

Leslie came right on her due date. Chuck's mother would take me to my doctor's appointments. She always said "Now, honey, I am not driving you to the hospital when the time comes. Chuck needs to do that."

I totally agreed with her. So, one day as Chuck's mom was driving me to my doctor's appointment, I kept having cramps so strong they made me stop talking.

Finally, Chuck's mom said," Honey, I think you're in labor."

"No, they don't feel like labor pains, I'm sure." How very naive of me!

When we got to the doctor's office, he said, "You need to go to the hospital. You're already dilatated five centimeters."

I was stunned. When I called to tell Chuck, he was so excited he put his lit cigar in a paper-filled trash can. It caught fire, but his co-workers took care of the fire.

Chuck's Mom did end up driving me to the hospital. I refused to go back with the nurses to get me set up to deliver, because I wanted to see Chuck before my delivery. In 1968, no one was allowed in the delivery room except the patient, the nurses, and the doctor.

We waited close to an hour while I was in active labor. Finally, they told me if I would go back and get set up to deliver, they would let Chuck see me once. His parents waited with him, and my parents arrived from San Antonio in time. Mother, Daddy, Charlie, Mary V, and Ken (best friend to both of us) had a party in the waiting room. Chuck paced the whole time, crying because he was concerned I was going to die.

Chuck's paternal grandmother died in childbirth, giving birth to his dad and his twin sister, Bertha. His grandfather was Charles Emil Praeger, a very renowned architect. His homes and buildings are on the historical registry in Victoria, Texas, and all over Texas.

Charlie and Bertha, the twins, were raised by Bertha's sisters while their father traveled building homes and businesses. Never knowing their mother was a loss they never got over.

My OB/GYN came in to check how far along I was. He thought I had hours to go before I was completely dilated so he left to go back to his office. I sat up, bent over my pregnant stomach so they could get the IV going and give me the epidural injection in my lower back. As they were giving me the injection, a large contraction came. The nurses checked me, and I had gone from five centimeters to ten in one contraction. My child's head was crowning.

They reached my doctor. He came running back to the hospital from the parking lot. Leslie came out with one push. Our daughter was born.

Leslie was five months old when I got pregnant with our second child. When it was time to give birth to our second child, Laura, I was only in labor for two and a half hours.

When I look back, I realize I was a drill sergeant raising our girls. When they were starting high school and going to be dating boys, I told them, "If you think birth control works, look in the mirror. If God wants you to have a baby, you are going to have a baby." Both my girls were conceived on "birth control."

When Leslie was going away for her first year in college, the car was packed, but I told her to sit down in the living room. I told her, "I need to repeat all the lessons we have taught you for your first eighteen years of life."

Emotionally I needed to repeat all the lessons one more time before she left to become the person she is today. She sat down respectfully and listened.

At the end I said, "Now there are two rules for when you are in college. One: If you get drunk uptown and have to crawl home, I do not want to know. Two: If I do not ask the question, I do not want to know the answer. What I mean by these statements is that I know you will make mistakes. But as long as you are safe and not in trouble, they are your mistakes to figure out."

To this day Leslie will tell me, "Mom, you know I never told you about such and such."

I will say "Did I ask the question?"

"No."

"Then I still don't want to know."

I also told my girls as they were in their teen years and beyond, "There is a loving and just God. Someday you, too, will have children."

My daughter, Laura, takes a picture each year of her daughter walking away from the house on her way to school. A very poignant picture. You see the back of the child walking into a world she will be involved in, her life. It is not your life. As her parents, you will be a part of her life, but you will not live it. In the end, it is her life.

MIRACLES

The first miracle was that Chuck and I met. From a joke to fifty-three years together. An incredible marriage! We were best friends, lovers, soulmates, everything. Throughout our marriage, many people told us, "I've never seen a marriage like yours."

The second miracle was Chuck getting into the reserves three days before our wedding. Many people might say, "That's just luck." I call it a miracle and God looking out for us.

Armco Steel

Chuck started with Armco in sales. We only lived in Houston for a year. Then Armco transferred Chuck to the corporate office in Middletown, Ohio. He was in training for sales. After three years, Armco decided to put Chuck into marketing/sales. This opportunity really grew his knowledge of metal buildings. For twenty-six years he was instrumental in building the metal building industry to what it is today. Over the years the company went from Armco Steel to Stellox to Kawada Industries.

Thomas Associates

In 1995, Chuck took a buy-out from his company, Steelox. We had a salary and insurance for one year. He wanted to take a year off to heal. Steelox had been sold to Kawada Industries out of Japan. Kawada instructed Chuck to put together a metal roofing division. The men he brought into his group were all loyal to Chuck.

For three years they had a cohesive group that collaborated well with each other. Then Kawada decided they did not want a roofing division, so they told him to fire the men in his group. Chuck was devastated for these men. One minute they had good jobs, and the next they were let go.

So, when they offered Chuck a buy-out, he took it. It was just Chuck, Denece, the two beagles, and a $200 per month house payment. We were good.

In October of 1995, we went to San Antonio to attend my nephew's wedding. Since I had a highly successful cake business out of my home, I took my cake pans with me and made the wedding cake.

When we got home from the wedding, we found a message from the president of Steelox, Chuck's former company. The message said, "Chuck, call me when you get this. I've recommended you for a job that I think you'll like."

Chuck called Frank on Sunday. Monday, he talked to the president of Thomas Associates in Cleveland. They flew him to Cleveland on Wednesday, hired him on Friday, and he moved on Saturday.

This was another miracle in our lives. We had printed out one hundred copies of Chuck's resume and never mailed one. The job he took was perfect for him. What he had done for one company, he would now be doing for the entire industry. He was vice president of Thomas Associates which manages trade associations. Metal Building Manufactures Association was their largest account.

Chuck was now General Manager of MBMA. The companies in MBMA were all competitors of each other. What Chuck had done for one company, he would now do for the industry. His job was to bring all the metal building companies together and merge them as one group, working for the same goals.

I was so excited for Chuck. When he was in high school and college, he studied to become a lawyer. Then he met me and gave up that dream.

After ten years of marriage, I asked him, "Do you have regrets not pursuing your dream of becoming a lawyer?"

"Absolutely not! I'm very happy with our lives."

At Thomas Associates, Chuck utilized all the things he had learned in college. He worked with all the different companies and the lawyers involved. He loved his job, the people he worked with and setting goals for the industry.

In 2014, Chuck was at work and not feeling well. His friends at the office noticed and took him to Lakewood Hospital in Lakewood, Ohio. Julie, the receptionist, called to tell me what was going on and where they had taken Chuck. He was sixty-nine years old.

When I got to the hospital, the new cardiologist, Dr. Angel, was sitting on the bed talking to Chuck. He asked him what he did for a living, and he very humbly answered. Then the doctor looked at me and asked, "What does Chuck do for a living?"

I told him about Chuck's work and how stressful it was. He was doing five people's jobs. Chuck never talked about the stress he was under.

Dr. Angel said, "Now there is the truth."

Chuck was diagnosed with restrictive pulmonary hypertension causing congestive heart failure, as well as atrial fibrillation. The first diagnosis meant he was having fluid buildup around his heart and would, from time to time, need the fluid drained, through a procedure called diuresis.

Atrial fibrillation meant Chuck's heart would go out of rhythm and they would have to cardio-avert his heart. Basically, stop his heart then start it again, hopefully in rhythm.

We both realized this was a death sentence. Our prayer was that God would give us many more years together. The doctors wanted Chuck to lose weight, exercise, and cut his drinking at night to just one. He was overweight and did not exercise but was not an alcoholic. We both just enjoyed having a drink together at night.

For me, this diagnosis was terrifying! Chuck was the love of my life, my partner, best friend, lover, soul mate, my everything.

At his one-year checkup, Dr. Angel commented, "I'm amazed he's still here."

I said, "Can you give me at least five more years?"

"I can't promise that, but don't worry, Denece, I'll find someone else for you."

"I don't want anyone else. I want Chuck. No one else."

December of 2014, at age sixty-nine, Chuck decided to retire. I always said to him, "You are blessed because only you will know when you are ready to retire." His company did not have mandatory retirement dates.

Thomas Associates gave him a wonderful retirement party. They even flew Laura in from Minnesota. For his retirement, we went to Hawaii for six weeks. I was so amazed and felt it was a miracle that Chuck was still with me.

Man of the Year

In April of 2019, I was in my sewing room and Chuck was in his office upstairs. He came into my room and said, "You're not going to believe this, but I've been nominated for Man of the Year in the metal building industry."

I said, "It's been five years since you retired. How do they even know who you are?" Sounds like a mean thing to say, but Chuck was as surprised as I was.

They flew us to Hilton Head in South Carolina for the award. We checked into the hotel and got unpacked. We went downstairs and saw so many of the people Chuck had worked with. Everyone was so gracious. We attended a number of meetings for their regular annual meeting.

When it was time to present Chuck his award, I sat in awe as I listened to all that he had accomplished with MBMA. I knew he worked hard but not to the extent of what he accomplished. Chuck was a humble man, and I was so proud of him.

We planned to take three more days just for fun. But the day after the award, Chuck woke up and was having trouble breathing again. So, we called for an Uber since we did not have a car. The driver, Stephen, picked us up and took us to the hospital. Stephen gave me his business card and told me to call him directly if we needed anything.

They admitted Chuck and he stayed in the hospital for three days. His congestive heart failure was making it difficult to breathe. They did the diuresis to get the fluid off from around his heart.

Stephen in Hilton Head was a miracle for us. He came to the hospital each night and took me back the next day. He even took us to the airport to fly home.

Stephen is what I call a "Godsend." He came into our life at just the right time, helped us, and went back to his own life.

Talking to Angels

During Christmas of 2015, we went to Minnesota to celebrate with Laura, Rob, Ellabei, and our cousins, Kathy, James, and Michael from North Carolina.

Chuck started to not feel well. He had to sleep on the couch sitting up because he was having trouble breathing. I called Laura to come downstairs. I needed her medical opinion to assess him. She said, "Mom, he needs to go to the ER to be checked out."

When we got to the ER, Chuck started sobbing. I asked him why he was crying, but he was crying so hard, he could not answer me. They checked us into a room, and the whole time Chuck cried. This was not normal for my Chuck.

When the doctor came in, she asked Chuck why he was crying. He could not answer her, either.

As I explained to the doctor about his heart problems, Chuck focused on the wall across from him. He cried and said things that did not make sense.

I called Laura and said, "You need to come up here and experience this with me." She came to the room and saw Chuck was having a conversation, looking at the wall and crying.

She sat by his bed and told him how much she loved him. She told me, "Mom, he's having an out-of-body experience."

It made sense. Chuck was talking to angels, telling them he did not want to go yet. We held hands and tried to figure out how we could help.

I said, "Chuck, I am here. I will not leave your side. I will always love you. I will not be angry if this is your time to go to God."

They took him for tests. When they brought him back, he had stopped crying, but he was exhausted. He said, "The angels were on the wall. I was crying because I did not want this to be my time to go. The angels were so real. They were right there. I saw my life before my eyes, and I was begging them that this was not my time to go."

The test results all came back as negative. What we thought was another heart incident turned out to be nothing. So, we could take Chuck home.

The miracle here was Chuck talking to angels for four hours. Laura and I were blessed to experience this event with Chuck. It was truly incredible to watch and a miracle to be a part of it.

I believe angels are all around us. Sometimes I can feel their presence. Other times, I just know they are there, watching over me.

A song by Alabama that says exactly what I mean, is *Angels Among Us*.

Is Today the Day?

Because of my chronic pain and Chuck's oxygen, we slept in separate bedrooms. To be able to sleep, Chuck needed the French doors in our master bedroom opened, a fan in front of the door, and the fan blowing overhead.

I needed the television on low so I could sleep. We both hated not sleeping together. Every morning, I woke Chuck up so we could have coffee. And every morning as I was walking down the hall, I asked "God, is today the day?"

Three years before Chuck died, we were having coffee when I asked him, "Is the way you are living your life now, the way you intend to live the *rest* of your life?"

This question must have come through God. I never would have thought of it. I believe strongly that we each need to live our lives as we see best.

Chuck was not trying to lose weight. He was not exercising, and he was drinking anything he wanted at night.

I needed to find out if he was intentionally living this way. Had he made a conscious decision to do so? He looked at me and said, "I don't know."

I let it go. Two years before he died, we were having our usual coffee and I asked him again, "Is the way you are living your life now the way you intend to live the rest of your life?"

This time he said, "Yes."

I said, "I will love you. I will hold you. I will be right by your side. I will not be angry."

I strongly believe we all deserve to live our lives the way we want to, especially as we are near the end of our lives. We had no clue how long Chuck would live, but I wanted him to enjoy every moment of it. To live a life where I was not yapping at him all the time because he was not doing what the doctors were telling him to do.

Live your life your way.

Travel

Chuck wanted to travel but I was very frightened. He wanted to go to France for a month and Australia for a month. All I could think of was that he would come home in a body bag. I was that scared.

Finally, I said, "Okay, let's try France. If we do that without a hospital stay overseas, then I'm in for Australia."

So, in 2018 we went to France for a month and had a terrific time. We started out in Marseille. We toured Notre Dame, Monaco, The Monte Carlo casino where I got a picture of myself playing the slot machines. Then we did a Viking cruise down the Rhone River, ended up in Lyon, and headed to Saint Malo.

In Saint Malo we stayed with a woman who rented out rooms in her home. Her house decorations were things she and her husband had found on the beach off Normandy. She had a huge plane propellor blade that was from a German plane from World War II. We walked on Normandy Beach and then went to Paris. In Paris we toured the Palace of Versailles, the Louvre Museum, and the Eiffel Tower. Chuck's health stayed good as well as mine.

In 2019, since we had done so well in France, we planned a month-long trip to Australia. We would be in Sydney for a week, Cairns for a week, then do a two-week cruise around New Zealand and fly home. The girls were concerned about the trip, but we promised we would fly one of them over if we got in trouble.

To get on the plane, Chuck had to get approval from his doctor as well as the airlines to take his travel oxygen. We got the approval, so off we went. I was not concerned about myself at all.

The flight to Australia was long, but since we flew first-class, we were comfortable. Our pod folded out flat so we could sleep. When we landed in Sydney, as we were deboarding the plane, I got very nauseous. I went into the bathroom and threw up seven times. When I came out of the bathroom, they put me on oxygen and called the EMT's. The EMT's took me down to the doctor at the airport to be checked out. He gave me nausea medication and sent us on our way.

At the hotel I tried to sleep but could not. I laid in bed for twelve hours while Chuck slept. He was so exhausted; I did not want to disturb him.

When he woke up, I told him we needed to go to the hospital. He drove me to the ER. They took us back to a room. I was coughing like crazy, had a horrible headache, and just felt awful. After eight hours in the ER, they finally told me I had Influenza A and admitted me to the hospital. I was so sick.

I called our girls and said, "One of you has to fly over and bring us home or I'm afraid I'm coming home in a body bag." Not the right thing to say to your daughters, but I was sick. Laura flew in to help us get home.

Because I was in isolation, Chuck could not see me. I was there six days. As they were moving me to my regular room, I had two grand mal seizures. I had never had a seizure in my life. After the seizures, I came down with Posterior Reversible Encephalopathy Syndrome (PRES) of the brain. I was in intensive care for five days. PRES is a rare condition where parts of the brain swell, usually because of an underlying cause. Symptoms present as seizures, disturbed vision, headache, and altered mental state.

When they finally released me, we needed to stay in the country for two weeks before they would release me to fly home. Laura checked my vitals twice a day. When she presented my blood pressure measurements to the hospital, they gave us the go-ahead to fly home. When we landed in Los Angeles I wanted to get down on the ground and kiss it. I was that happy to be home.

The miracle here is that I did not die, as sick as I was. God still had plans for me. It took a good four weeks before I had my energy back.

Falling Down the Stairs

The last week of July in 2020, Leslie and her best friend, Jen, came to visit Chuck and me. Their visit was an annual trip for them. Jen, Leslie, and Chuck would spend the week talking and sharing their spiritual quests together. Jen noticed that Chuck was struggling. He was very pale, struggling to breathe, with little energy, huffing and puffing. The girls tried to convince Chuck that he needed to go to the hospital. He refused to go.

On Friday of that weekend, we were in the kitchen preparing dinner together. Chuck and I had two songs that said everything we felt about each other. Celine Dion's song *Because You Loved Me* and Lee Ann Rhimes *How Do I Live Without You?* Which suddenly came on the radio. Chuck took me in his arms, and we danced to the song and held each other tight.

I am so grateful Leslie recorded the dance on my phone. When I watch the video on my phone, I can still smell and feel Chuck. I did not know it would be the last time I would ever dance with my Chuck.

After the girls left, I finally convinced him to go to the ER and be checked out by the hospital staff. They admitted him for diuresis again.

Chuck was in the hospital five days. I stayed with him during the day. I called my best friend/sister to drive up from Dayton, Ohio to help me take care of our dog, Sydney. I would come home from the hospital at night, then go back the next day. On the morning of the fifth day, I told Val to call the EMT's. My chronic pain was over the top and I could not get out of bed. Since my chronic pain started in 2006, I had never gone to the hospital for my pain. That morning, I just could not move. They admitted me to the hospital. Chuck was on the fourth floor, and I was on the fifth floor.

The next day they were releasing Chuck and me at the same time. Val came to pick us up. We got home, and I still had pain medication in me. Because of all my surgeries, I had what I called 'Denece's medical equipment' in our basement. We were all watching television in the guest room, when Chuck commented that he wanted the raised toilet seat I had in the basement. Without saying a word to Chuck or Val, I got up to go to the basement to get the toilet seat.

I got to the end of the stair railing with my hands on the railing, when I could see myself passing out. The room was going black. I assumed I would pass out on the floor by the rail. Val watched me flip over the rail, do two somersaults, three flip flops, and land on the hardwood floor at the end of the fourteen steps.

On the last step, I looked down at my body lying on the floor. I can still remember the conversation I was having with God as to whether this was my time to die. And I felt the whoosh of my soul reentering my body.

I do not remember the EMT's or the five days in the hospital. Leslie stayed with me in the hospital. The next memory I have is being in a Hoyer lift to get me in my bed at rehab. A Hoyer lift is a cloth with chains on each end to lift you up. The EMT's transferred me from the ambulance to the fabric of the lift to get me into bed.

With the T-six fracture and the fracture in my sternum, I was screaming my head off. One of the rehab people took a pillow and doubled it over, bound it with tape, and told me to hug the pillow for the pain. It worked very well. I hugged that pillow anytime they had to move me.

I was in rehab for six weeks. While I was healing, Leslie and my dear friend Nancy came up to see me and be with Chuck. They helped Chuck get a chair lift put in for me for our stairs and arranged a hospital bed for when I came home. They also had a very rough talk with Chuck.

Leslie told Chuck that my falling down the stairs was his fault for not taking care of himself. She told Chuck that I did too much for him. By not taking care of his condition, he was putting me at risk as well as himself. His decision was impacting the entire family.

One day, I was in the hospital bed in our family room, and Chuck was in his chair. We were watching television, and I asked Chuck, "What has to happen for us to make the decision to move out of this big house?"

He looked at me and said, "Honey, don't worry about it. It's all going to work out." I think he was aware of his pending death.

The Miracles at the End of Chuck's life

On October sixteenth Leslie came in to spend time with us. She came in on Friday and we had a great time, talking, laughing, and just being together. Leslie had not seen me since I had come home from rehab. Around seven, I needed to go upstairs and get in bed to rest my back. Leslie and Chuck stayed downstairs to have dinner and be together.

I crawled into bed. As I was watching television, I heard loud music coming from the kitchen. I muted the TV and listened. They were making dinner, having margaritas, and dancing to Michael Jackson's *Off the Wall*. This was so fitting for the two of them.

When Leslie was in eighth grade, Chuck drove Leslie and her friend Robin from Dayton to Cleveland to see Michael Jackson in concert. The girls had a terrific time and Michael Jackson became a staple in our home. We all loved his music. So, listening to Leslie and Chuck singing and dancing warmed my soul.

About 11:00 that night, they came up and went to bed. I was already sound asleep in my room. At 2:15 a.m., I got up to go to the bathroom and noticed the overhead light was on in our master bedroom. That was odd. I went into the hall and started walking to our master bedroom. I was also talking to God and asking him, "Is this the day?"

As I was walking down the hall, I passed the master bath. I looked in and saw Chuck lying on the floor on his stomach with his head turned to one side.

I yelled for Leslie, and she came running. I checked for vital signs but could not find any. We rolled him over and Leslie started doing chest compressions. I called 9-1-1, put Sydney (our dog) in her crate, and opened the front door. But I knew when I could not find a pulse that Chuck was gone.

The EMT's came and worked on him for about fifteen minutes. Then they loaded him into the ambulance.

I was in shock and not thinking clearly. Leslie drove us to the hospital, and we went in through the ambulance bay. Normally you cannot go that way, but the nurses were wonderful. They let us through. They said, "Mrs. Praeger, just sit here and the doctor will come and talk to you."

I could see them working on Chuck and I knew he had been down too long for them to bring him back. He had said good night to Leslie at eleven o'clock, and I had found him two and a half hours later.

The doctor came out and said "Mrs. Praeger, I'm sorry but he's gone."

Leslie and I went in to see him. I went by his side, held his hand, and laid my head on his chest. I cried so hard. He was my everything. I did not know how I was going to live my life without him.

We called Laura and Rob. The hospital called a minister to say last rites while we held Chuck's hand.

Leslie and I finally went back to the house around four o'clock in the morning. I do not remember if we tried to go back to bed, or what we did. It is all a blur. Laura flew in the next day.

The first night that he was gone, Leslie told me he came to her in her sleep and said, "Leslie, Leslie, I got my wings!"

When we went downstairs to make coffee and try to wake up, a red hand towel was on our black granite countertop. The towel was folded neatly, and in the center of the red towel was a white feather. We did not own any feather pillows in the house. Chuck had left it for us.

Because of COVID, we were not able to have Chuck's service at our church. So, we held it in our backyard, the backyard he loved so much. Chuck would always find God in our backyard, so it was perfect to have the service there. Our minister came to do the service and be with us. The day was a beautiful October day. The sun was shining, and we could feel God's love. We had planned a celebration of Chuck's life the next year, but again, because of COVID, we cancelled it.

As I have been authoring this book, more miracles have happened. I write in my den and have a day bed in there. I went to write one day, and the daybed was completely empty of any papers. I looked down and there was a letter Chuck wrote to me on my 65th birthday. I do not remember ever seeing this letter:

My dearest sweetheart, July 27, 2013

Congratulations on reaching the grand age of sixty-five, I thought I would never get you here. It is such a milestone in more ways than you know. As a matter of fact, it will be revealed to you through insights, whispers and loved ones throughout the year.

You have been in my heart for all eternity and just think, we destined this life to join ourselves together to take one hell of a journey. And one hell of a journey it has been! When I saw you standing at the door on Lilac Lane, the lights went on, and they have kept burning brightly ever since. I'll never forget as we stood together to join and had two beautiful babies, daughters, and how life-giving it was for both of us. At that moment, it was our purpose.

It was so wonderful to bring our families together in marriage and to celebrate life's moments with Sueatis, Dewitt [my parents), Mom and Dad, and our sisters and families and friends. In memory it feels like a large warm blanket. Like a home with joy and sadness but most of all a state of full being.

Your unselfish love, light-heartedness, and sunshine have been everything to me, and you have reflected that to me every day — even on those dark days. I know you have lived with so many physical conditions that would have put me under. Your courage, persistence, and spirituality have been a beacon for me. I can never express my deepest appreciation for the patience you have shown me throughout our lives.

I am so proud of you, of who you are, what you are, where we are together, and our life journey. It's been so much fun, and I can't wait for the fun to continue.

Happy birthday, sweetheart, and let's go on skipping together forever.
Love, Chuck

The Celine Dion song "*Because You Loved me*" was our song. We would play it and dance to it. The song meant everything to me, everything Chuck did for me. He married an eighteen-year-old innocent girl and helped her to become a mature complete woman. I am so grateful I left the earrings in his pocket.

As I looked back, I realized that for six months, he had been dying right in front of me. He did not want to die in a hospital, but at home. Chuck would say, "I want to go out of this house feet first," and that is exactly what he did.

THE MANY MIRACLES IN OUR LIVES

- *Meeting Chuck on a blind date and getting married one year later.*
- *Chuck getting into the Army reserve three days before our wedding.*
- *Finding the letter he wrote to me in college. I had scrapbooked all the letters he had written me. Then as I was writing this book, that letter showed up in the middle of my cutting table.*
- *The two passages from Kahlil Gibran on how we wanted our marriage to be and how we planned to raise our children.*
- *Chuck joining Thomas Associates without sending out a single resume.*
- *Chuck getting Man of the Year, five years after he retired.*
- *Talking to angels.*
- *I recovered fully from PRES while in Australia.*
- *When Leslie and Jen came to visit, Leslie taking the video of Chuck and me dancing to our song. I treasure the video so much.*
- *Telling Leslie that he got his wings.*
- *The white feather on the kitchen towel.*
- *Finding the letter, he wrote to me on my 65th birthday.*

HEMINGWAY

The same year that Leslie was born, my dad (Daddy) retired from the Army. Growing up, I was very close to my dad. My senior year, Susan was in college, Beverly was married, so at night, while mother worked, we would talk. He would talk to me until four in the morning and then call the school and tell them I was sick and would not be coming to school that day. I graduated from high school with a 'C' average, having never cracked a book. Daddy talking to me all night, was an early sign of his mental illness.

The gift of our conversations was that I could honestly say I knew my dad. I learned what his goals in life were, what his disappointments were, and what his growing up was like. That time with him is still precious.

In 1968, San Antonio was renovating the downtown and the river that ran through San Antonio. This included building HemisFair '68 which was the first and only World's Fair to be held in San Antonio, Texas. The six-month celebration was proposed by local business leaders to commemorate the 250th anniversary of the city's founding, and the shared cultural heritage of San Antonio and its Latin American neighbors.

After Daddy retired, he was looking for something to do. So he signed up to help build HemisFair. Before HemisFair was completed, we were never allowed to go downtown by ourselves. San Antonio had seven military bases and it was not safe for young girls.

Once HemisFair opened, it really changed the dynamics of downtown. Once the River Walk was developed with restaurants, hotels, and shops, it became a destination city. San Antonio has so much to offer tourists.

In August of 1968, Chuck and I decided to drive in from Houston with our two-month-old baby. Daddy sent us off to enjoy the fair while he babysat Leslie. I have a wonderful picture of my dad holding Leslie.

What follows are several miracles I experienced when Daddy did something that shocked us all.

Right after that weekend, Daddy and Bob, a buddy of his from the Army took off for a trip to Costa Rica. Bob and Daddy did many unique trips. During the Cuban Missile Crisis, they went to Colorado to go hunting. They were gone for a week and Mother had no way to contact them. They were flown in by helicopter and would be picked up by helicopter once the week was over.

Now they wanted to go to Costa Rica. Mother had no idea how long they were going to be gone. As they were gone longer and longer with no contact, the family concluded that Daddy was not coming back. He had gone eight months without any contact with Mother.

I was the baby in the family, and I could not believe he would just take off and not communicate with me. I cried while Chuck held me. At that point, we all started grieving the loss of our dad. Maybe this was just another wild thing that my dad did, but this time, he was not coming back.

Chuck was working for Armco Steel Company, and I was home in our apartment with Leslie. We were renting furniture, so we decided I would go back to work and save the money for us to buy some furniture. I started working at a savings and loan as a receptionist. Going to work every day helped me not think about the loss of my dad as much.

Our next-door neighbor, Ronnie, made it possible for me to be able to work. She was a God-send in our lives. She agreed to watch Leslie while we both worked. She had a son a little bit older than Leslie, so it worked out well for her as well. The first miracle with my dad was that Ronnie was there to take care of Leslie.

One day we came home from work, and I went next door to pick up Leslie. Ronnie had her ready for us, but she also had a package for us. When I opened it, there was a note and a cassette tape. I went straight for the tape, but we had no way to play it. We did not have a cassette player.

Ronnie had a machine that would play it, the second miracle. So I went back to our apartment and as God would have it, we played the wrong side of the tape first. Daddy was talking about the trip and how much fun they were having. Then we opened the letter:

"16 February 1969

Dear Chuck, Denece, and Leslie,

The trip here was rough and more expensive than I thought. Bob could not rough it like I could. He had to stay in air-conditioned hotel rooms. So that has run me short of money for the return trip home.

Bob is going on to Panama tomorrow and returns to San Jose Monday the 23rd of February. He has to have his Jeep worked on, which will take two or three days. I have plans to leave San Jose, Monday 2, March 1969.

Could you send me $600 so I can get back home? I will repay you in two months' paydays. If so, send it to The Bank of America in San Jose, Costa Rica.

Miss y'all a lot and hope I can be home for our wedding anniversary. I'm in a jam but nothing like before. No hot checks or the like. Just need funds for the trip back.

Love, Daddy"

Hearing my dad's voice for the first time in eight months stunned me. I had been grieving him for months and here he was talking to me on the tape. I was in shock. Now my dad was asking us for money, or he would be in jail if he didn't have it in three days.

In 1968 it was unheard of to wire transfer money. We had the money, but Chuck's dad always taught us not to touch our savings. So he lent us the money. Then we had to figure out how to transfer it to Costa Rica. Chuck's dad was friends with the president of the bank, and they were able to get the money to my dad.

Somehow, we found out what flight number he was coming in on. Mother came into Houston from San Antonio and was as shocked as we were. She had been grieving the loss of the love of her life. Mother stayed with Leslie while Chuck and I took off for the airport.

I can still remember the shock and how panicked I was. Panicked because I had no idea how to greet my dad and act as if nothing was new. As we drove to the airport, Chuck held my hand and gave me support. I had accepted that my dad was dead, now I was going to see him in person.

I remember, as if it was yesterday, walking down the concourse toward his gate. Back then you could still walk to the gate to greet people as they got off the plane. But when I looked up, Daddy was walking toward us. He was smiling as if this was nothing. He looked like Hemingway, the writer. He had a beard at least twelve inches long and was wearing a one-piece jump suit just like Hemingway.

Daddy hugged and kissed us, like this was no big deal. I was over-joyed, confused, and shocked that my dad was standing in front of me.

We drove back to our apartment. Daddy walked in and kissed my mother like I had never seen them kiss. They packed up and drove back to San Antonio.

We lived in Houston until July of 1969. When Leslie was only five months old, I got pregnant with our next daughter, Laura. Armco wanted to send Chuck to their corporate office in Middletown, Ohio. They gave us the option of staying in Houston until Laura was born or moving while Laura was still in my tummy. I voted to move while I could hold one daughter's hand and have one child in my body.

We moved into a townhome in Middletown, Ohio, near Armco's plant. Daddy came up to stay with me for two weeks while Chuck did his two weeks Army reserves. Daddy was there with me when Neil Armstrong walked on the moon, a particularly important event for America. I was so grateful Daddy was with me.

Laura was born within two and a half hours from the first contraction to delivery. Leslie's birth took five hours. Our girls are only fourteen months apart.

After Laura was born, we moved into a rented house in Middletown. One time Mother and Daddy drove up to visit in their Winnebago. Chuck and Daddy were unloading the stuff they had brought us while Mother and I were having coffee in the breakfast room.

The phone rang. It was my mother's best friend, Jo Hickman. She lived across the street from my parents' house. Jo had a daughter, Joann, who was a couple of years older than us. Joann had given birth to a daughter, then died right after the birth. Jo called mother for comfort. When Chuck and Daddy found out, they started packing up Mother and Daddy's stuff because they were driving back to San Antonio to be with Jo.

All my life, my mother never verbally told me that she loved me. She always showed it but didn't speak the words. I looked at my mom and said, "I love you so much, Mother."

She was crying and said, "I love you, too." It was the first time I had ever heard those words from my mother. I always heard "I love you" from my dad. What she said was amazing. I asked her why she never told us she loved us.

"I was so afraid you wouldn't say the words back."

I learned something that day. We can judge someone, but we do not know what their lives have been like. We only see what they show us and there is so much more. We only saw our grandparents in North Carolina once every four years. There were no interstate highways, only two-lane highways. We did not have the money to fly. So, I really had no idea how my mother was brought up.

After this incident with Joann, Mother and I always said, "I love you."

After three years in our rental home, we built our first home in Germantown, Ohio. It was a nine-mile drive for Chuck to the office. I was a stay-at-home mom. To buy our home, we had to put down ten percent of the cost of the house. Our home cost $31,500 to build. We had the $3,100 to put down on the house, but Chuck's dad said again, "You don't touch your savings for anything."

Chuck's dad lent us the money. He charged us eight percent interest. Our friends were stunned that he would charge interest, but we always said, "He is losing eight percent interest on his money. Of course, we are going to pay him back interest."

I went to work at Barnitz Bank in Middletown as a teller. We only had one car, so Chuck dropped me off on his way to work and picked me up on his way home. As soon as I made the $3,100, I quit and went back to being a stay-at-home mom. Chuck and I went on to live our normal life in Germantown.

After the incident in Costa Rica with my dad, we discovered he was a manic depressive (bi-polar). Bi-polar is a disorder associated with episodes of mood swings, ranging from depressive lows to manic highs. After Daddy was diagnosed, we looked back at our lives growing up and could see his highs and lows. In 1973 this was a new diagnosis. As a family, we did not understand it. Even Mother had not studied manic depression in nursing school.

One day in 1978, Daddy called me at home and said, "I am calling a family meeting for 5:00 pm tomorrow. If you are one minute late, do not bother walking in the door."

We called American Airlines and booked two tickets for the next day. The girls stayed with their babysitter, Wanda.

We flew into San Antonio the next day getting in at 4:30 p.m. Chuck's mom and dad lived about five minutes from my parents. We rang the doorbell, and I thought, *"Gosh, I hope we don't give them a heart attack!"* They had no clue we were coming. We used their car to drive over to Mother and Daddy's place.

When we got there, Mother was sitting on the couch. Susan, and her husband, Ned, Beverly, and her husband, Bobby were already there. Susan and

I sat together on an ottoman. I remember vividly that I just wanted to melt into the corner of the room.

My dad was miserable with his life. This misery was caused by his manic depression. He called the 5:00 meeting to help him get out of this misery. Chuck and Bobby started negotiating with Daddy, producing all kinds of solutions for my parents' lives. Daddy kept saying the solutions would not work. Mother just sat there and said nothing. She was in shock.

Finally, they produced a solution that Daddy agreed with. We would help Mother and Daddy get a divorce and set them up in their own homes.

As we were leaving, Daddy looked at Chuck and said," You will never accomplish this."

Chuck said, "Dewitt, just watch me." It does not sound like it, but Chuck and my dad were remarkably close. Chuck loved my parents.

We drove back to Chuck's parent's house. I do not remember if we even ate dinner. I went to bed, shocked at what was happening.

The next morning, Chuck's dad came into our bedroom, "Chuck, you need to get up. We have a problem."

I went back to sleep. A little later, Chuck's dad came in and woke me up. He said, "Honey, you need to get up and get dressed. Come out to the breakfast room."

I did as I was asked with no clue what was going on. When I got to the breakfast room, Chuck was on the phone talking to the Terrill Hills police. Terrill Hills is a suburb in San Antonio where my parents' home was. Chuck was asking the police what to do with my dad after he picked him up.

When he got off the phone, he told me what was going on. "Honey, your dad is lying in bed with a loaded gun by his side. He says if I do not stop him, he is going to kill your mother and himself. Call your sisters and meet me at this attorney's office with your mother in about two hours."

Bobby came and picked Chuck up. They drove to Terrell Hills. Bobby stayed in the car with a police car parked in front of him, but the police car was not visible from the house.

Chuck entered the house from the back door and went into Daddy's room. Mother was asleep in her room, oblivious to what was happening. Daddy was dressed and lying in bed with the loaded gun. Chuck calmly took the gun from my dad and told him to come with him. They walked to the car, Bobby drove while Chuck and Daddy sat in the back seat.

They drove to Bexar County Courthouse. Chuck and Daddy sat on a bench outside the court doors. Daddy seemed to come out of it and realized where they were. He turned to Chuck and said, "Chuck, don't do this."

"Dewitt, we are doing this."

Daddy said, "You've changed the rules of the game."

They entered the judge's chambers. All Daddy would say was his name, rank, and serial number. The judge committed my dad to the state mental institute for two weeks. They took Daddy away, and Chuck met us at the lawyer's office. Mother had to sign the divorce papers.

Then Chuck said, "Come on everyone. We are going to see Dewitt." He had promised Daddy that we would not abandon him. Chuck drove with Mother in the front seat and Susan, Bev, and I in the back seat. I can still remember feeling how I wanted to mold into the corner of the car. I was petrified to see my dad in an institution.

When we arrived, Chuck came to get me, and I pulled back. "Please don't make me go in there."

"Honey, don't worry. He'll be in his room. You will not see him right away." I was the first one to enter the institution. As I went through the door, he was right in front of me, two feet from me.

He looked at me and said, "How could you do this to me?"

He turned and walked away and went to his room. I was devastated. We were going to leave but I spoke up and said, "I have to go to the bathroom."

Mother said, "Denece, you have to go every time you even see a fire hydrant."

Chuck decided to go with me to keep me steady. We had to ring the buzzer at the nurse's station for them to buzz us in. I went first and then stood outside the door while Chuck was in the bathroom. As I was standing there a doctor walked by, stopped, and then backed up. He took my hands and said, "Are you Mr. Reynolds' daughter?"

"Yes."

"You did the right thing. Your father would have killed your mother and himself. You saved their lives." His statement helped me let go of the guilt I felt. The doctor was another God-send.

We all went back to my parent's house. Chuck was collaborating with the attorney to start the process of divorcing my parents. Before Chuck and I flew back to Ohio, I went to visit my dad. I went back to his room, and he was sitting on his bed. The last words I had with my dad were an argument. I never saw him alive again. I never got to say goodbye to him and tell him how much I loved him. I still have regret. I did not get to tell him what I had learned from him and the gifts he had given me in my life.

When we were home again, it had been two weeks since Daddy had gone before the judge. Again, he just stated his name, rank, and serial number. That bought him a month. They moved him from the State Mental Institution and into the Army's Woolford Hall, a military psychiatric unit. If he had gone before the judge a third time and just stated his name, rank, and serial number they would have committed him for a year.

Beverly and Bobby saw him every day and brought him whatever he needed. But no one had medications to treat manic depression. It was a new mental condition.

While Daddy was in Woolford Hall, he received the divorce papers. This was November of 1978. He looked at the divorce papers and had a massive heart attack. Fifty percent of his heart died that day. That fifty percent was the love he had for my mother. He loved my mother so much, he could not live without her.

As I reflect on this memory, my parents had a very deep love. In 1942, my mother had just graduated from nursing school. Pearl Harbor happened and one of the doctors from Mother's school decided to put together a medical hospital of 350 nurses and doctors. Mother joined the unit from North Carolina, and Daddy joined the unit as a med tech from Big Sandy, Texas. They met in Macon, Georgia.

The entire unit was deployed to San Diego, California where they boarded the USS Uruguay, a cruise ship. The 350-person unit bordered the ship. They found out in Tasmania where they were going. They were given a 4x6 booklet on the customs and language of India. They landed in Kolkata (Calcutta) and traveled by boat, railroad, bus, and convoys to get to Assam. They were part of the China-Burma-India campaign. Mother would say they took care of the "Fly Boys, flying the "Hump." The airmen were flying across the Himalayas to bomb Japan. I have pictures of my mother squatting in a trench where they would transfer the patients when the Japanese bombers flew overhead.

Mother and Daddy were in India for three years. They got married March 14, 1945, in Assam, India by the Church of Scotland. They had their honeymoon on a houseboat in Kashmer, India. Daddy would tell us, "They broke the bed making Susan." When they discovered mother was pregnant, the army sent her back to North Carolina. Daddy did arrive in time to be with Mother for Susan's birth.

The last few days of his life, he became our dad again. He apologized to Bev and Bobby for all the antics he had done. He became the sweet, wonderful dad we grew up with. I was happy that Beverly and Bobby were with him when he died. I still have regret that I was not with him to hold him and be able to say how much I loved him.

Chuck and I were sitting at dinner one night and I told Chuck, "When the call comes in that Daddy died, I do not want to be the one to answer it."

The next night, the call came at dinner. I got up and left the table and went to our bedroom. I knew it was "the call." Chuck came in to tell me and sat with me while I sobbed. We caught a flight out the next day. The girls were only nine and ten, so we did not take them with us. Once we got to San Antonio, we rode in the car with Bev and Bobby and me crying over our loss. Beverly was able to share Daddy's last days with us.

After the way Daddy died, I told Chuck, "I will never let this happen to me again. I do not care if I spend every dime we have, I will be with my family when they die."

Daddy's death changed the course of my life on how I responded with my loves ones as they were dying.

THE MIRACLES IN THIS STORY

- *I got my dad back after eight months of believing he was dead.*
- *I found the letter that Daddy wrote to us, fifty-six years later.*
- *Ronnie lived next door to us and babysat Leslie while we were at work.*
- *Ronnie had a tape machine that played Daddy's tape. Back then hardly anyone had a tape player of any kind, much less one that would play this specific tape.*
- *The miracle of Mother telling me she loved me.*
- *Chuck walked in on my dad while he had a loaded gun by his side, and Daddy did not pull the trigger.*
- *Meeting Daddy's doctor at the mental institution after I went to the bathroom. He helped relieve me of the guilt I felt from putting Daddy in an institution.*

"I DIED LAST NIGHT"

In July of 1995, when I told Mother about Beverly's stage four, level four, breast cancer diagnosis she looked at me and held up her index finger. "I will not bury one of my girls."

I told Susan and Chuck, "Mark my words, she will die before Beverly."

After the miracle with Linda, the angel, and getting Beverly moved to San Antonio, Mother set Bev up in her own apartment just down the street from her condo.

Bev could drive herself to her chemo treatments, the grocery store, etc. She got to spend time with her daughter and her granddaughter. Her daughter was also pregnant with another grandchild. We had someone to help her when she needed it. But after six months living alone, Beverly was declining from her cancer.

Mother told Susan and I that she wanted us to move Bev into her condo to live with her. We both argued strongly that Mother wouldn't be able to take care of her. Bev had always been thin, never fought a weight problem. But now with the chemo she had put on a lot of weight.

"Mother, you can't even lift her thigh. How are you going to take care of her?"

But Mother had to try taking care of her daughter, knowing full well the effort would probably kill her. Again, she refused to bury one of her daughters. Mother was insistent. So Susan and I helped Bev make the move into Mother's condo.

Mother had a custom bed made for Bev that was electric like a hospital bed. A twin bed would be too small and a full-sized bed too big, so this was three-fourths size. We wanted Bev to be able to put books, papers, and anything else on the bed, so she did not have to reach for it.

One day we had one of those absurd moments. We were putting Bev's clothes in the closet, which would have filled three closets. Susan was putting up Bev's wigs and caps and stuffing them in because there was no room.

Beverly very quietly said, "You know, Susan, I think if you give it a little more effort, you will be able to ruin every wig and cap I have."

Bless Susan's heart. She lost it and ran out of the room crying.

Bev had been at Mother's house for three months when Bev called and asked me to come to San Antonio and put her in the nursing home. Bev's calling me was a big deal. Holding a phone was very painful for Bev because both of her arms were fractured from the cancer.

I called Susan so we could meet at Mother's, then I caught the next flight out from Ohio.

When I walked into Mother's condo, she was sitting in her chair while Bev was in her Relax-the-Back chair. Susan and I went to the love seat. We started discussing the issue of Beverly going to the nursing home. We all knew this would be her last move before going to God and her place in heaven.

Susan and I argued and yelled at each other. Susan tried to come up with other solutions. "I'll move her to Houston and take care of her."

Beverly just sat in her chair and looked at Susan, then me. For the entire time we argued, Bev looked from one of us to the other, never saying a word.

Quietly, Bev said, "Susan, it's time."

Susan and I started sobbing and holding each other. We went out to the patio and sobbed and sobbed. When we finally could talk again, we agreed. We knew it was time for this final move.

We called Parkland Nursing Home to see if space was available. They said, "Yes," so Susan and I got Bev ready for the nursing home.

She lay in her bed and told us what she wanted to take with her. Everything had to have her name on it, even her underwear, so we labeled all her clothes.

It was so hard for all of us. Beverly had come to acceptance, but Susan and I still struggled. We did get her settled in her room at Park Lane. She was in skilled care and still receiving chemo. But the chemo could not defeat the cancer.

When I flew back to Ohio, I prayed for God's strength to get me through this loss. This was my constant prayer.

I was not home even a day when Mother called and said, "Denece, I need you to come to San Antonio and put me in the hospital. I have pneumonia."

Needless to say, I called American Airlines and caught the earliest flight out the next day. Because I was going to San Antonio two weeks out of every month, the ladies at American Airlines knew me and would ask, "Denece, what is going on now?" When I told them, they were all so empathetic it felt like a hug.

They put me in first class again. As we were flying south, I looked out the window and prayed for God's strength to get me through.

When I got to Mother's condo, I was shocked at how thin Mother was. We had all been so focused on Bev, we weren't looking at what this was doing to our mother. I took Mother to the ER.

She looked at me and said, "I am not going to do another endoscopy." Mother had survived stomach cancer for eleven years. Being a nurse, she knew what her symptoms meant. She was sure the stomach cancer had come back.

She kept telling me she was not going to have any more tests run. That lasted until her doctor came into the room. He sat on her bed and said, "Now, Sue, you know you are going to let me do the endoscopy."

She said, "Yes."

When he left the room, she said, "Isn't he just so cute?"

I told her, "When he comes back, I'm going to tell him you have a crush on him."

"Don't you dare!"

I did tell the doctor and Mother blushed. She was just so precious about it all. As they wheeled her out, I kissed her and told her how much I loved her.

She said, "I can't believe I'm going to have this test done." Then with a sparkle in her eye she said, "Just think, Denece, I might die on the table."

"That's right, it *could* happen that way."

When they brought her back after the procedure, she came to from the anesthetic and said, "Shit, I'm still here."

Mother's doctors and Susan tried to convince her to do chemo again. I sat on the extra bed in her room as she looked at me, rolled her eyes, then looked at them again for about ten minutes.

She finally looked at me and said with her index finger raised, "I will do *one* round."
Everyone was so happy. They left to go start the process.

Mother looked at me and said, "I can't believe I'm going to let them do chemo on me again."

I told her how much I loved her and then said, "Just think, Mother, the first round could kill you." (I have a sick since of humor, and so did she.)

"You're right!" she said with a smile on her face.

Again, I remembered her words, "I will not bury one of my daughters!"

Mother's last days were when I realized the process of dying is between God and that soul. You can kick, scream, or yell all you want. But you do not get a vote. It is between God and that soul. If you are lucky, you get to be a part of it by holding their hand, rubbing their back, or just sitting with them.

They admitted Mother to the hospital to start her on the chemo. I stayed with her during the day and hired Alissa, to stay with her at night. Having been a night nurse, Mother would "turn on" at night and want to talk. Alissa was there to get her anything she wanted and listen to her.

I spent the days with Mother. She talked about her life and how she was ready to go. Mother and Daddy both donated their bodies to the University of Texas Health Science Center. Mother said, "Denece, they are going to learn so much from me." She had only a fourth of her stomach due to stomach cancer, scoliosis on the upper portion of her spine, and gastric esophageal reflux disease. She was thrilled to help the incoming med students as a cadaver.

On the third morning I came in to relieve Alissa who said, "I don't know what is going on with your mother. She is all a twitter about what happened last night."

"Don't worry, I'll talk to her."

Alissa left and I sat down next to Mother. She was quite excited. "Denece, Denece, I have to tell you what happened. I died last night!"

"Mother, you didn't really die last night. You might have gone to the precipice, but you didn't go over."

"Would you shut up? This is my story."

I drew my finger across my lips to seal them shut.

She started describing heaven to me in vivid detail. "Everything was silver: the houses, the street, the leaves on the trees. It was so beautiful, but I looked around and no one was there to greet me."

Then God said, "Sue, you have to go back."

"I don't want to go back. I want to stay here."

"It's not your time yet."

So, Mother came back. But she had this beautiful glow about her. I was in awe.

They moved Mother to a Telemetry Unit where there was one nurse for two patients. While she was there, she slowly lost her ability to speak. She was having small strokes and was down to one-syllable words.

Mother lay at the head of the bed. Susan was at her side, and I was at the foot of the bed. This doctor we did not know, came in and flicked one of the bags that was hanging with her meds in it. He said, "Well, I see that the medication that she is getting to stop her body from shooting the small blood clots, is working."

My mother's eyes got huge as she glared at me. I looked at the doctor and said, "What do you mean, she's getting medication to stop her heart from shooting the TIA's! She's a *no code*!"

As the doctor and I yelled at each other, Mother's oncologist came in. "Denece, what are you yelling about?"

"Mother is a no code! Why are you giving her medication to stop her heart from shooting the TIA's that is part of the process of how her body is shutting down?"

We argued some more. Then with tears in his eyes, he asked my mother. "Sue, are you ready to go home?"

"Yes."

He looked at me and said, "I wasn't ready to let her go."

I was still heated and responded back, "That is not your decision to make. This is between God and my mother. You don't get a vote."

He looked at Mother again and asked, "Sue, are you sure you are ready to go home?"

"Yes." Then she focused on me and kept saying, "Ask him."

He had both hands on the rail of her bed when he turned to me. "Denece, what does she want you to ask me?"

"I don't know, I've been arguing with you and not focused on her."

I looked at Mother. She focused on me and said, "Ask him."

"You want me to ask him about Beverly?"

"Yes."

I said, "She wants to set up a fund for women who cannot afford tests for breast cancer. She wants to know if we can set this up on the south side of town or the north side of town."

He looked at Mother with tears in his eyes. "Sue, that's what you want to know?"

"Yes."

With his head down, he said "I'll help you set this up on the south side of town where it is most needed."

That day we moved Mother to a private room. She was slowly dying so we gathered the family around her. We literally had a wake in her room. Someone was touching her the whole time. She would look up and see everyone there and she would smile. We ordered pizza and played card games. This went on for three days.

As I watched Mother, I could literally see her life going out of her eyes. She had dark brown eyes but as she was dying, I saw the light fading. Her eyes were turning to light gray.

The family left because once Mother was moved home to Hospice, we did not know how much longer it would be. She could have three days left or a couple of weeks.

I had a flight out to Ohio the day she was going home. Susan would be the one to move Mother back to her condo for Hospice.

As we were waiting, I held her arm and she held mine. Our arms were locked while she slept.

Donna, the head nurse came in and said, "Denece, I don't know what is keeping her here. You've done everything to help her transition home."

I said, "I can tell you exactly why she has not passed away. She refuses to die in this hospital. She will die at home."

At that point, Mother let go of my arm. That was the sign I needed.

I had been sleeping in Mother's bed at her condo and was talking to God all the time. I was struggling, trying to decide if I would stay in San Antonio and help Susan transfer Mother home or go back to Ohio.

As we let go of our arms, I finally felt that God was helping me to decide. I did not need to see my mother take her last breath.

Susan needed to be the one with Mother. I was prepared for Mother's death and Beverly's death. Susan was not.

When Susan got Mother home, Mother focused on the corner of the room, smiled and said "Sarge." Sarge was our dad's name. She was going home to so many of her family that were there to greet her.

I did fly out that day. American Airlines again had put me in first class. As we flew, I looked out the window at the clouds and blue sky. I continued with my prayers to help me handle all that was going on. My prayer this time was "God, please give me strength."

I flew into Cincinnati, and Leslie picked me up at the airport. When we walked into her house, the phone rang. It was Susan. Mother had just died.

I looked at Leslie and said, "Come on, we're going shopping. This suitcase will not make another trip." Leslie and I both thought this was humorous. Through all the deaths we were going through, we had to find the humor to make it through or be a basket case and non-functioning. Going "shopping" was funny.

We both flew back to San Antonio the next day. When Chuck flew in, we went to Porter Loring Funeral Home to make the arrangements for Mother's viewing.

When the director came into the room, he excitedly told us he had taken every urn they had for Beverly to pick the one she wanted. She disliked all of them. But he recently got a new one in and took it out to Bev. She loved it, so he was pleased.

When he showed it to us, I started crying. The urn Beverly chose was identical to the one Daddy had made me for Rainbow Girls. It was an altar all hand-carved with beautiful trim all over it. I really felt Daddy had helped Beverly pick the perfect one.

We arranged for Mother's viewing at Porter Loring, with her hands across her chest. She looked so peaceful and at rest.

After the viewing, the family gathered back at Mother's condo. Beverly sat in her Relax-the-Back chair in the living room. This chair is an 'S' curve. It really helped Beverly to be comfortable because it took the pressure off her spine.

This was September. I looked at Bev and asked, "What is keeping you here?"

She looked me directly in the eye and said, "Nece, I want to see my grandson born and have Christmas with my family. Then I am out of here."

Susan, Chuck, and I planned Mother's service. She wanted to be buried at Fort Sam Houston with our dad. This would take place a year later. When you give your body to science, they have the body for one year while the incoming med students work on them to learn the human body.

During that year, Susan and I cleaned out Mother's condo and sold the three condos she owned. In July of 1997, I called the University of Texas Health Science Center, to check on where they were in the process with Mother. Shirley, the contact person paused for a long time.

Finally, I said, "Shirley, I have a very sick sense of humor. Just where exactly is my mother in the process?"

Shirley said, "Well, your mother was such a unique case we held her over for a year for the incoming med students." Mother died in September, but the med students do their cadaver in August of their incoming year. "I hope we have not offended you."

"No, Shirley, you just made Mother's day. She wanted to be a cadaver for the medical students."

As I watched Bev and Mother die, I realized that no matter how much I screamed, kicked, got angry, cried, or yelled, I was not a part of the process. It was not about *me*. This was completely between their soul and God. I did not get a vote. This was hard to accept, but once I did accept it, I realized they were giving me an incredible gift. It was their time to go, and they were asking me to be a part of it. To hold their hand, get them anything they needed, to easily pass, to gather their loved ones around them and help them on this journey.

Mother's journey was the most incredible experience I have ever gone through. It was better than giving birth to my children. I would go back and do it all again with her. She was so ready to die and not afraid at all. She talked with me every day about it and was so peaceful and serene. She trusted that I would be there with her and to be her advocate with all the doctors and hospital staff. She gave me the privilege of holding her hand while she went to God. She gave me life and I got to hold her as she went to God. What an incredible gift! I would not have missed it for anything.

If you get this chance, stop your world and take the chance. It does not come around very often.

MOTHER'S MIRACLE

The miracle with Mother was her going to heaven and talking with God as to whether it was her time to go or stay.

Another miracle was that I could stop my life and be with my mother as she went to God.

LIGHT ON THE RINGS

In 1995, I was going back and forth to Colorado and then San Antonio a week to ten days of every month. Most of these trips were not planned trips. I would call the airlines, mostly American Airlines, and say, "I need a ticket, and I need to be in San Antonio or Colorado tomorrow. I do not care where I sit on the plane, just give me a seat."

More than half the time American Airlines would put me in first class. When I was on the plane, I would look out the window and talk to God for most of the flight. My prayer was, "God give me strength."

In September of 1996, Mother died. As I was flying back and forth to be with Bev and to start cleaning out Mother's condominium, God said to me, "Do you understand you are strong?"

I heard His voice. It is hard to describe in words. His voice, for me, was more feeling His presence all around me. But when He said, "Do you understand you are strong?" It was a firm, strong voice.

Chuck's mother died in November 1996, at Thanksgiving. Mary V. had Pick's Disease, a form of Alzheimer's. Pick's disease affects the frontal lobes of the brain and is much shorter than Alzheimer's, normally seven to eight years. The difference between Alzheimer's and Pick's disease is that a Pick's disease patient will look at, for example, a key. They know it opens something, but they cannot tell you what it opens, or that the name is "key." They can look at a piano and know that it makes music, but they cannot tell you it is a piano.

On that plane trip I was praying to God to give me courage. We flew into San Antonio and had the service at the Presbyterian Church for Chuck's mom. Chuck's dad was at Parkland Nursing Home. With a caregiver, he was able to attend the service. After the service, the family flew to Dallas.

Most of the Praeger family will be interned at Restland Cemetery. We had Mom's interment in the Garden of Love, the Praeger plot. Harvey and Bertha Chamberlain are interned in the Garden of Love. Bertha was Chuck's dad's

(Charlie) twin sister. Their only child, Jayne died in a small plane crash in Peru. Jayne is buried at Restland as well. Chuck and I will be beside Jayne. So now Mom was interned. Chuck and I will be buried there someday along with his dad.

When we flew home from Dallas, I was praying for courage. I heard God's voice again as He said to me, "Do you understand you are courageous?"

I prayed some more and this time I said, "I understand, there is only one set of feet in the sand, and they are not mine." I was in God's hands as we continued to give Bev as good a life as we could.

While packing up Mother's house, I made piles for Chuck and me, Leslie, Laura, Susan, Tres, and Ryan. During all of this activity, Beverly was fading.

In December of 1996, at Christmas, I told our girls that I needed a break from all the deaths, illnesses, packing up, etc. I wanted to go on a cruise. To get away and just float on the ocean without my grief being the only thing I could think.

I asked the girls if they wanted to go with me. Leslie was working for Procter and Gamble, and Laura was in residency. If they would join me, I would pay. They could pick where we would go, because I did not care. "Just let me get a break from my life."

They decided on the Caribbean. We left on the trip in January of 1997. I do not remember where we went or all the things we did. But every night we had dinner with the same couple, Trisha and Michael. They lived on the east side of Cleveland, and I was on the west side.

One night before we were going snorkeling, Trisha and I were talking about our wedding rings. I said, "I never wear my rings when I snorkel in the ocean."

Trisha and Michael were travel agents who traveled all over the world. Trisha said, "I always wear my rings and have never had a problem."

The next day we were on an exclusive island for the cruise line. The girls and I snorkeled in the morning. It was so soothing. I love water — to just float and look at beautiful coral and fish was exactly what I needed.

After lunch, we sat on the beach enjoying ourselves. The girls were reading and basking in the sun. After a little while, I got up to go to the bathroom. When I came back Leslie said, "Mom, you are bad luck."

"Why am I bad luck?"

"Because Trisha lost her rings in the Caribbean!"

"Come on, put your mask on. We're going to help Trisha and Michael find her rings."

"Mom, you are *not* going to find those rings in the ocean."

"I am *not* getting back on that boat having not tried!"

So I swam out to where Trisha and Michael were. Trisha was crying. She just could not believe the rings came off her finger. I asked them to show me where they had been in the water. I told everyone, "Let's divide up to find her rings."

We each took an area. As I was putting on my snorkel mask, I started praying, "God, shine the light on the rings."

When I put my face in the water this beautiful light went all the way down to the sand. God was shining his light on the rings. They were floating, standing up together, and swaying with the movement of the water.

"Michael!" I called. He swam over and dove down to get the rings. Trisha was so thrilled. We were all in awe.

MIRACLES

Finding Trisha's rings in the Atlantic Ocean.

Talking with God and hearing His voice.

GO TO THE LIGHT

When we were growing up, we were "The Three Reynolds Girls." Susan was the oldest, Beverly was born one year later, and I was born eighteen months later. We were remarkably close.

Mother and Daddy's friends always said to us, "Susan is the smart one. Beverly is the pretty one, and Denece has the personality. Put them all together and you have the perfect person."

But that taught Susan that she was not pretty and had no personality. Beverly was not smart and had no personality, while I was not smart and not pretty. It took us years to realize this was not true.

When I was fifty-seven and finishing The Cleveland Clinic's Chronic Pain Management course, my counselor told me how smart I was. "You could be in Mensa," she said. "Mensa is an organization of just ordinary people with extremely high IQs who tend to be very curious, quick to grasp concepts, and have many widely varying interests. Most Mensa's have a good sense of humor, they like to talk, and usually have a lot to say."

That evening, I came home and sobbed on our couch. When Chuck came in from work, he asked, "Why are you crying?"

"Because of the report on my IQ. I realized what a waste of a brilliant mind. I could have done so many things, but never thought I could."

Our family was medical. Mother was a pediatric night nurse, Daddy worked in the medical field at Fort Sam Houston, Susan was a nurse, and I worked for a doctor. My youngest daughter, Laura, went to medical school to become a doctor. Around the dinner table growing up, we always talked about medicine.

Beverly had a rougher life than Susan and me. She had a husband that played around on her and a contentious relationship with her only child. It seemed like everything Bev touched did not work out. Everything Susan and I touched turned to gold.

I was a homemaker for most of my life. This was a choice and a decision that Chuck and I made at the beginning of our marriage.

As a homemaker, I made all my daughter's clothes, Chuck's suits, and my clothes. I cooked, canned vegetables, went to co-ops for home-grown fruit, vegetables, and home-churned butter. I upholstered furniture, made drapes, and decorated our home.

When our girls graduated from high school, Chuck said to me, "If you want to go back to college, we have the money."

There would have been three of us in college at the same time. I wanted to be a doctor. I said, "That's twelve years of school! I would be fifty and just starting out."
Instead, I worked for our local doctor for seven years and loved every bit of it.

Beverly was not medical at all. She was a paralegal. After Beverly's divorce, she bought a house in Terrell Hills, Texas. The plan was that her daughter would pay her rent so that she and Bev's granddaughter could live with Beverly. Bev planned that the rent money her daughter would pay, would go into a college fund for her granddaughter. They had a huge falling out. Beverly sold her house and moved to Colorado Springs, Colorado.

To find God again, Bev chose Colorado Springs. By February of 1995, she had a job, a place to live, and finally — medical insurance. With God's help, she was healing emotionally.

In July of 1995, Susan's oldest son, Tres, was getting married in San Antonio. Chuck took a year sabbatical from his work, so he and I flew in for the wedding. For twelve years I ran a cake business in my home, including wedding cakes. So I brought my cake pans with me and was delighted to make Tres and Cyndi's wedding cake.

We were at my mother's when the phone rang. It was Beverly. I answered the phone.

She said, "Nece (my nickname) I'm not coming to the wedding. I have breast cancer."

I started crying and went into the living room away from our mom. Chuck took over the phone and talked to Bev. When I finally had myself back together, Chuck gave me the phone and Bev said, "Nece, why are you crying? I'm just going to lose a breast. So what?"

She was right. That was not so bad.

Then she said, "Nece, tell me what these words mean, *metastatic degenerative extensive bone cancer?*"

Again, I sobbed, and Chuck took the phone from me. He talked to Bev until I could get myself back together. When I could talk again, I said, "Bev, I need you to send me those reports."

In her innocence, she said, "Do you want me to send the bone scans as well?"

"Yes, honey, send me everything. Go to Kinko's to overnight them to me. I'll pick them up tomorrow and send them back to you soon."

After the conversation with Bev, I went into the den to talk to our mother. I told her "Beverly has breast cancer, and it has spread to her bones." This was one of the hardest things I have ever had to do.

Mother did not cry, but she looked me straight in the eye. With her index finger raised she said, "I will NOT bury one of my girls."

I told Chuck and Susan, "Mark my words, Mother will die before Beverly."

Our mother had been a survivor of stomach cancer for eleven years. I knew Mother's oncologist well from going with her to appointments. I called her oncologist and Reece, the receptionist answered. I told her about Beverly's situation. "When I have the films and reports, could I come over and ask the doctor to tell me what we are facing. I'll pay the doctor for his time."

Reece, said, "Just come over when you get the paperwork and films. You don't need an appointment. He'll see you when you get here."

I started baking the wedding cake and making the icing, trying to focus on putting the cake together, decorating it as perfectly as I could. It helped me to find something else to focus on.

The next day the papers arrived, and I drove to the doctor's office. I gave the test results and films to Reece. She then called me to go back into his office. He looked at the films and paperwork for about ten minutes, put them on his desk and said, "Denece, she has maybe a year to a year and a half to live."

I thanked him and went out to the car to cry before I had to tell Mother the news about her daughter. I can still cry about it, because I felt so awful. Beverly's dying was going to be a huge loss for our family.

When I told Mother and Susan, they were both shattered. But we all needed to buck up and enjoy Tres and Cyndi's wedding. I finished the cake, and we took it to the church to set it up. We came back to Mother's, and we all got dressed for this beautiful wedding. We did not tell Tres and Cyndi the news until after their honeymoon.

After the wedding, Chuck and I flew home. Within two weeks, I began my trips back and forth to Colorado. From 1995 to 1999, I was gone one to two weeks out of every month. None of the trips were planned.

American Airlines got to know me well. I would call on one day and say, "Get me on a plane tomorrow. I don't care where I sit. Just give me a seat." More than half the time, they put me in first class. During all the many flights to help Bev, I looked at the sky out the window and prayed. "God, give me strength."

Bev and I prepared for what was to come. We went to a wig store to buy a wig and caps for when she lost her hair. She also wanted to get her hair shaved and not wait for it to fall out. I watched them shave her head and was amazed at how emotionally strong she was.

I went to doctors' appointments with Bev to be her second set of ears, because she did not understand what they were talking about. Through this experience with Bev, I learned everyone needs a second set of ears when you go to the doctor, especially if it is hard news to absorb.

When I arrived at the hospital in Colorado, I first went to the chapel to pray. I felt myself putting my emotions on a shelf to deal with later. It was not going to help Bev if I was crying all the time. I really tried hard to give her a cheerful outlook.

They did a double mastectomy and told her she was a candidate for an autologous bone morrow transplant. Autologous bone marrow transplant is where they take stem cells from the bone marrow in your hip, clean it up, then transplant the new cancer-free cells back into your body. Bev would be in isolation for about six weeks to keep her from getting any illness. Later we found out she was *never* a candidate for this bone marrow transplant. Her cancer was too widespread. She had bone cancer from the top of her head down to her toes.

Susan wrote grants at a Houston hospital. She had a harder time stopping her work life to go help Bev. I worked part-time for our local doctor in Germantown, Ohio. He was so wonderful to let me take off at a moment's notice, making dozens of trips from Ohio to Colorado or San Antonio.

Susan and I were with Bev for the mastectomy. When she was released to go home, we brought her back to her apartment. We rented a hospital bed and got her set up in her bedroom. Susan had a flight out that day and my flight was the next day. Susan made a list that she taped to the wall by Bev's bed for the signs to look for that would indicate she was crashing.

Crashing Signs

- Bleeding that will not stop
- Breathing problems
- Change in mental status
- Chest Pain
- Choking
- Coughing
- Vomiting up blood
- Severe or persistent vomiting
- Severe pain
- Inability to speak
- Bluish skin color
- Unusual headache

Bev and I were watching a movie in her bedroom when I could see her crashing in front of me. She could not focus on the movie we were watching, was having trouble breathing, and she was very unsteady. I said, "Honey, I'm sorry, but we have to go back to the hospital."

I helped her dress and got her walker. She was so weak. Somehow, I got her down the eight steps from her apartment to the ground floor. I got her to the curb of the road and said to her, "Stay. Please hold on to your walker and concentrate on not falling into the street."

Petrified that she would fall before I could get there, I ran to get her car. I helped her in and took her to the Emergency Room. They took her back right away and admitted her. Bev was as safe as I could make her, so I flew back to Ohio. Twelve hours after being home, the hospital called and said, "If you want to see your sister alive, you need to come now."

I called Susan. She turned around and flew back to Colorado. I flew back, praying all the time for God's healing for Bev and for God to make me strong to help her.

When we got to the hospital, her room was right by the nurses' station. When you are as fragile as Bev was, the nurses want you close to them.

Susan and I decided we would divide up Bev's care. I cleaned Bev from the waist up while Susan had the waist down. We tried hard to find the funnies in the whole situation. The absurdity of what we were dealing with was all surreal. If we could not have found those funnies, we would all have just cried constantly. That would not help Bev tackle her life-threatening situation.

When the doctors admitted her, they discovered her lungs were filling up with fluid. They took her downstairs for a procedure called thoracentesis. They would go into her lungs and draw out the fluid to see what was causing her lungs to fill up.

Susan and I went to lunch. When we came back, Bev was not in her room. Susan stopped at her door and froze. She asked the nurses where they had moved Bev. They told Susan she was at the end of the hall. Susan looked at me with her eyes wide and said, "Nece, she's going to die."

"We know that."

"No, very soon."

"How do you know that?"

"Because they move patients that are terminal with not a lot of time left to live to the end of the hall to give the family privacy. Also, the nurses do not respond as quickly as they would if she was right next to the nurses' station." Even though we knew she was terminal, it was a shock to realize Bev's death was imminent.

We walked down the long hall and found Bev lying in bed, struggling to breathe. Her lungs were filling with fluid. They had her on medication so she would be comfortable, but it really was a matter of days or hours before she would pass. While Susan and I were with Bev, she kept begging us to kill her, to end her excruciating pain.

Watching Bev in so much pain brought me back to an earlier memory of pain I experienced. When I fell off a ladder at twenty-seven, I herniated five disks in my lower back. I told myself that if the pain ever got so bad that I could not deal with it anymore, I would take my own life.

Here was my sister begging us to do exactly that. We had the means to do it. We had just filled 360 morphine tablets and 360 Percocet pills. Clearly enough to take her life.

But all the while Bev was begging us, God kept saying to me, "So you think you can do it. Can you do it? Can you give the pills and kill your sister?"

I finally realized I could never do it for Bev or myself. Bev's begging us went on for thirty-six hours non-stop. We talked to the doctors. They gave her more medicine to make her more comfortable. She was already on a nasal cannula giving her oxygen through her nose. They finally gave her as much oxygen as they could. But bottom line, her lungs were about eighty percent filled with fluid.

By this time, Susan and I were exhausted. My youngest daughter, Laura, was in medical school so she took time off and flew in to see her aunt one more time. When she got to the hospital, she said, "Mom, Aunt Susan, you need to go get some sleep. I'll stay with Aunt Bev."

We both were struggling whether we should leave or not.

Laura finally said, "Do you really need to see her take her last breath?"

I realized I did not. I was so grateful that Laura had come, and I knew Bev was well cared for. Susan went to tell the nurses we were going to leave and that Laura would be with Beverly. I was standing outside of Bev's room and heard Christian music playing in the next room.

A woman came out of the room. She came up to me, took both my hands in hers, and said, "Hi, my name is Linda. I hope the music is not bothering your sister. Tell me the story of your sister."

So, I did. She asked if we could go and pray with Bev.

"Of course. Bev would love that. She came to Colorado to find God again."

We went into Bev's room and formed a ring around the bed. Beverly was at the head of the bed, I was at one side, Linda was at the foot of the bed, and Laura was on the other side. Linda said the most beautiful prayer I have ever heard. It was all about God's healing. A prayer that Beverly would continue to live life on this earth or healing where she went to God and was no longer in pain. When Linda finished the prayer, I thanked her and joined Susan so we could get some sleep.

At 7:00 the next morning we were back at the hospital for the doctors' morning rounds. We got off the elevator and the entire nurses' station was all a twitter. Everyone was talking all at once.

Susan and I looked at each other and said, "What is that all about?"

We walked down the hall to Bev's room where three doctors stood outside her room. They were in as much of a twitter as the nurses. Susan went in to see Bev.

I asked the oncologist and the two pulmonologists, "What's all the hullabaloo about?"

Dr. Huffman looked at me and said, "Denece, I can't explain it, I just can't explain it."

"What can't you explain?"

"Her lungs are clear."

I had seen Bev's x-rays from last night that showed her lungs were eighty percent filled with fluid. He showed me her new films and her lungs were clear. He was just beyond words.

Then he said, "You wanted three days to get her back to San Antonio. Well, you got them."

I went in to see Bev, and she was sitting up in bed with only a nasal canula for oxygen in her nose. She was eating breakfast and talking to Laura and Susan. When I came out of Bev's room, I noticed there was no Christian music playing in the room next to her. The room was empty. I started looking for Dr. Huffman. When I finally found him, I asked him where the woman in the room next to Bev had gone?

He looked puzzled. "There was never anyone in the room next to your sister."

"No, her name was Linda." I described her to him. "She was about five foot three inches, brown hair, and so warm and calm. She held my hands."

He shook his head. "There was never anyone in that room."

"So, what you are telling me is that we are witnessing a miracle?"

"Denece, a miracle is the only thing I can call it."

I was amazed! Bev's miracle was happening right in front of us. After the miracle with Linda, everyone went into high gear to get Bev home. The nurses started working on what I called the "Apollo Space Mission." Within three days, they had it all worked out so we could get Beverly back to San Antonio.

Chuck flew to Colorado to drive Bev's car. Susan stayed in Colorado to pack up her apartment and stayed until the movers arrived. Then Susan flew home. Bev and I flew first class on American Airlines. The EMT's picked us up from the hospital.

One of the EMT's said to me, "You can sit in the front as long as you don't touch any buttons." It was so hard not to touch anything just from curiosity, but I was good.

They took us to the airport and put Bev on a gurney to take her to the gate. We all rode in the cart with Bev between us. I looked at my watch and said to the lady driving the cart, "We need to call ahead to tell them to hold the door for us."

She said, "Oh no, they never hold the door for anyone."

"Oh, I'm sure they will hold the door for us because that is her next round of oxygen."

She called ahead and they held the door.

The EMT's got Bev in her seat in first class and hooked up to oxygen. The flight attendants were so nice. Bev slept, and they asked me if I wanted anything to drink.

"I'll take a mimosa and keep them coming, I'm not driving."

We had to change planes in Dallas. The EMT's met us at the gate, loaded Bev on another cart, and off we went to the next plane. We were the last ones on again, and the EMT's hooked her up to her next round of oxygen as they brought me another mimosa. When the plane landed in San Antonio, we were the last ones off the plane.

As the plane was deboarding, every single person on that plane touched Bev's shoulder and said, "I will pray for your sister."

At the hospital, they settled Bev into her room. I called Mother so she could finally see her daughter. When Mother arrived, I did not go in with her. This was a private moment just for the two of them.

Bev's new oncologist came to see her, and I remember vividly hugging her medical records to my chest. He needed me to give them to him, but I was petrified to let go of her records. I was handing him Bev's life.

When Mother knew we were moving Beverly back to San Antonio, she rented an apartment near her condominium. Chuck came in with Bev's car, and Susan came in to help us get Bev set up in her new apartment.

When they released Bev from the hospital, Mother and Susan helped Beverly move into her apartment. They hired a caregiver to be with her in the daytime. The caregiver would take Bev to her chemo appointments. Bev could manage on her own at night.

Chuck and I flew back to Ohio. When we got home, we checked the answering machine and there was a message from his old boss. Chuck was taking a year off to regroup on his career. The message said his old boss had recommended Chuck for a job at Thomas Associates in Cleveland.

Chuck talked to the president of Thomas Associates on Monday, they flew him to Cleveland on Wednesday, and he accepted the job on Friday. He moved to Cleveland on Saturday. I had a house to sell, a hysterectomy to live through, and I had to find a new home in Cleveland. I did not make the move to Cleveland until six months later.

After six months of Bev living on her own, I was back in San Antonio again. Mother was insisting that we move Bev into her condominium. Susan and I fought strongly against this idea. Bev had never fought a weight problem, but the chemo had put weight on her. We said to Mother, "You can't even lift her leg!"

Mother was adamant. She was going to take care of her daughter. I knew this was going to kill my mother, but she wanted to do this so that she would die before Beverly. She repeated, "I will not bury one of my girls!"

Susan and I cleaned out Bev's apartment. Bev had every piece of clothing she had ever owned. When we moved her into Mother's condominium, we stuffed all of Mother's closets with Bev's clothes. She had so many scarves and hats to cover her bald head.

Looking at the packed closet, Bev said, "You know, I think if you put in little more effort, you will accomplish ruining all of my head pieces." We all started laughing at the absurdity of the situation.

Through all of this, I developed a sick sense of humor. I would laugh at the surreal things that were happening to us. It felt better to laugh than to cry all the time.

Bev stayed with mother for three months. Then one day in July of 1996, Bev called me. It was difficult for her to use the phone because she had a fracture in both arms. She said, "Nece, it's time for you to come down and put me in the nursing home."

We all knew the nursing home would be the final stage of her life. Susan and I arrived and talked with Bev and Mother. Susan argued like crazy for us not to do this. She even offered to bring Bev to Houston and take care of her. Susan kept arguing with me.

Finally, I said, "Susan, you are trying to kill the messenger, Beverly is asking for this, not me."

The whole time we argued, Bev just listened. She would look at Susan and then me for at least an hour. Finally, Beverly said, "Susan, it's time."

Susan lost it and went outside, sobbing. I joined her, and we cried together. We all knew this was Bev's last move before she would die. We started planning to take Bev to Park Lane Nursing home. It was close by, and Mother could see her.

With Bev in Parkland Nursing Home, Mother started getting sicker and sicker. Bev living with her had accomplished exactly what she wanted. Mother was determined not to bury one of her daughters. Mother died in September of 1996.

At the same time, I was cleaning out Mother's condominiums, I was going to see Beverly at Parkland Nursing Home, always checking to see if I needed to do anything for Beverly. She was due for her six-month MRI, CT scan, and bone scan to see where the cancer was in her body and to see if the chemo was doing any good. These tests were so incredibly painful for her with all the bone fractures.

Bev arrived at the testing facility by Medi cab, in a wheelchair. I was sitting there, waiting for her to arrive. She wheeled in and looked at me with panic on her face.

I said, "What is the matter?"

"I think I really messed up."

"What do you mean?"

"I got a letter notifying me that my insurance is going to be cancelled."

My heart sank. "Did you bring the letter? Why would they cancel you?"

"Yes, I have the letter here. I forgot to pay my COBRA payments for the last three months."

I could not believe what I was hearing. My heart sank, but I tried not to show panic on my face and tried to just breathe. I sat there with Bev as long as I could stand it, then finally said "Hon, I have to go. I must try to see what I can do about this. I'll talk to you later this afternoon."

Bless her heart, she looked at me, just devastated, and said, "Nece, I am so sorry! I have really messed things up."

"Don't worry. I'll get this fixed. You worry about you. I'll take care of the rest."

We were packing up Mother's condominium to get ready to sell it, so I drove back there. We still had furniture, electrical, water, phone service, etc. The two things we did not have were an answering machine or cell phone. In 1997, cell phones were not as prevalent as they are today. Mother never had an answering machine, and I was not going to buy one for the limited amount of time I would use it. In hindsight, I should have.

I called Chuck at the office and cried. What were we going to do? Bev's monthly bills were:

                Nursing home - $3,000
                Pharmacy - $10,000
                Oncologist - $15,000
                Miscellaneous - $2,000

Her bank account was down to $20,000. With insurance, she was responsible for twenty percent. Without insurance, she would be responsible for all of it.

We had no idea how much longer Bev would live. Her oncologist continued to give her weekly chemo treatments. The chemo was strictly palliative care, not producing a cure for her aggressive cancer, but only making her as comfortable as they could.

I called Bev's insurance company. They directed me to the case manager. As "luck" or "miracle" would have it, she picked up. I was beside myself. It was my fault for letting Bev pay the most important bill she had. How could I have thought it was a good idea to have her pay this bill? With the morphine she was on, she could not concentrate on anything, much less pay her copay. Because she missed three months of the COBRA payment, they had the right to drop her from the insurance plan.

I explained everything to the case manager who said, "Let me work on this and I'll call you back."

"Okay. I'm going to see if I can get her on Medicare or Medicaid."

I gathered all of Bev's papers, birth certificate, SSI papers, and insurance papers and drove to downtown San Antonio to the welfare office. I took my place in line and waited an hour to finally talk to someone. We sat down and I explained Beverly's situation. They looked Bev up in the system but kept coming up with no way to help her.

Bev had just turned fifty that December, so she was too young for Medicare. She had to spend all her money down to $1500 to be eligible for Medicaid. Since we started her on SSI (Social Security Insurance) she would never be eligible for Medicaid. The $960 she received each month from SSI was more than she was allowed to make for Medicaid. The social worker looked through all the government programs but could not find a single program that would help Bev. She fell through the cracks.

I left there crying, not knowing what we were going to do. It looked like the only answer was that we, the family, would have to kick in to pay her bills.

When I got back to Mother's condominium, I called Chuck to tell him about the news from the welfare office and tried to figure out what to do next.

As the "miracle" (God) would have it, the phone rang. It was the case manager calling me back. She told me if I would send a check for $1800, Bev's three-month charge for COBRA, her insurance would be reinstated.

"I will overnight mail you the check this moment. You will have it tomorrow."

This was a definite miracle. I really could not believe it. Even after the miracle in Colorado with Linda, I was not recognizing God's work in Mother or in Bev.

In December of 1996, when I came back from a trip, I was rested with a new energy level to accomplish what needed to be done. I was still flying to Texas each month. There was still so much to do. Cleaning out Mother's condominium was a major task. Plus selling the three condominiums she owned, and I started the process of settling Mother's estate.

Susan and I had decided to divide and conquer. She would be the main contact for Beverly's estate while I would do Mother's.

Beverly continued to go downhill. She mostly lay in bed and watched television. She had a horrible bed sore on her right calf. The bed sore occurred because the nursing home had so much difficulty getting her out of bed. There was no skin on her calf. You could see the tendons and ligaments. She also had a bed sore on her right heel. They had her right leg propped up to not touch the bed and let air try to heal it.

I spent as much time with Bev as possible. "Honey, what can I do for you?" I asked.

One time she said, "I would really like a bean burger from Sils Snack Shack." A Sils Snack Shack burger had meat, refried beans, and Frito's on it. It was delicious. We always ate these hamburgers when we were in high school. They were unique to San Antonio.

Each time I saw Bev, she looked worse. She was slowly losing her ability to talk. I could see her dying before my eyes. It had always been "Susan, Beverly, and Denece." Now it was going to be just Susan and Denece — an excruciating reality.

In March of 1997, I was back in Cleveland, when the phone rang at 2:00 in the morning. It was one of the nurses from Park Lane Nursing Home. He said, "Mrs. Praeger, it's time to say goodbye to your sister."

I sat straight up in bed, woke Chuck up and said, "You mean now, right now, she is dying?"

"Yes, I'll put the phone to her ear so you can say goodbye."

I said, "Bev, go to the light. God will be there to greet you as well as Mother and Daddy."

When Bev spoke, it was totally garbled, and I could not understand her.

Chuck and I went into his office to call our girls so they could say goodbye. Later, Leslie called us back and said, "Mom, call Aunt Bev again. I could understand her!"

So I called again and said, "Honey, go to God's light and be with Mother and Daddy."

She said, "Nece, I see the light. I love you. I'm going to the light."

"I love you and I just want you free of the excruciating pain and in God's heaven."

Bev died March 18, 1997. We had her service at Alamo Heights Presbyterian Church in San Antonio, Texas. Her ashes are in the urn identical to the altar our dad had made for me when I became Worthy Advisor in Rainbow Girls.

THE MIRACLES OF BEVERLY

God tested me about taking my own life. I could not do it for Beverly and realized I could not do that for me either. When you die it is between God and your soul. No one else gets to vote. You can kick, scream, rant, and yell. But only the soul and God get to make the decision of when you die.

Linda, the angel in the hospital.

The Miracle of the Case Manager and the insurance.

The nurse calling to tell us Bev was going to the light.

FINAL GIFTS

After Beverly was diagnosed with stage four/level four breast cancer, I went back to Ohio and back to my job at the doctor's office. One of my coworkers, Gloria, gave me a book titled *FINAL GIFTS: UNDERSTANDING the SPECIAL AWARENESS, NEEDS, and COMMUNICATIONS of the DYING* by Maggie Callanan and Patricia Kelley. This book helped me tremendously.

It taught me the signals a dying person gives as they are nearing death. When you can recognize the signals, you can be a part of your loved one's passing. Because of this book, I was able to be with my mother, Chuck's mother and dad, and especially Beverly. I wish I had known about the book when my dad passed. I was not with him, and I have always regretted that fact.

Since I first received the book, I have purchased at least 150 of them. It has become a calling for me. God tells me when to buy ten more books and each time the ten books just fly off my bookcase. Many people have offered to give them back to me, and I always tell them to pass them on.

From the book blurb on the back cover, "Through their stories, we come to appreciate the near-miraculous ways in which the dying communicate their needs, reveal their feelings, and even choreograph their own final moments; we also discover the gifts of wisdom, faith, and love that the dying leave for the living to share."

Through all four deaths I experienced from 1996 to 1998, Mother, Mary V. (mom), Beverly, and Charlie (dad), they all did everything listed in the book although they never read the book.

After Beverly was moved into Park Lane Nursing Home, we knew this would be her last move. She called me one day and asked me to have Mother and Susan give her permission to die. I had already done that because of the book. I told Bev she had *my* "permission to die." I told her to go to God.

It was so painful for me to watch her in constant excruciating pain. It never let up. She had fractures in both arms, her hip, and her legs. The cancer was everywhere. I told her she did not need to fight this cancer and the excruciating pain for me. I wanted to see her out of pain with peace on her face.

After Bev's phone call, I called Mother and said, "Beverly needs you to give her permission to die."

Mother said, "I don't know how to do that."

I said, "I left a book on your coffee table. I know you won't read the whole book, but just read the last chapter, *'Nearing Death Awareness: Practical uses,'* and it will tell you how to do it."

Mother read the last three chapters, then went to see Beverly. She called me when she got home and said, "Well, I did it. Are you happy now?"

"Mother, Beverly asked you to do this, not me." I knew she needed to yell at me, not Bev.

It took Susan a lot longer to tell Bev. Susan is a nurse and felt that if she gave Bev permission to die, she would be killing her.

I never intended to leave the book on the coffee table. It was another of God's miracles that I left it. You could call it "happenstance", an "accident" or a blessing but I call it a miracle. God working through me to help Bev.

MIRACLES

Learning about this amazing book.

Leaving the book on Mother's coffee table.

All of us giving Bev permission to die.

MY JOURNEY WITH CHRONIC PAIN

In 1973, we built our first house. It was a basic bi-level of 1900 square feet with three bedrooms, two baths, a living room, dining room, kitchen, family room, and laundry room.

We lived in a small town of 5,000 people in Germantown, Ohio. It was a farm community where our girls could ride their bikes to the pool, the library, etc. Everyone knew everyone. Our house cost $31,500. We had the down payment of $3,100 in our savings account, but Chuck's dad taught us, "You don't touch your savings."

We decided I would go to work so we could pay Dad back. I took a job as a bank teller. We only had one car, so Chuck would drop me off on his way to work. Then he picked me up on his way home.

Wanda was recommended to us through the elementary school principal. She became a part of our family. The girls loved going to Wanda's. The girls were four and five with immediate friends and playmates — the other children Wanda took care of.

The whole purpose of my job was to pay off the loan we had with Chuck's dad. We even paid him eight percent interest. Many people could not believe we were paying interest. But we said, "Why not? He's losing eight percent interest on the money he lent us."

I worked at the bank for ten months. As soon as the loan was paid off, I quit. Chuck and I had agreed early on in our marriage, that my job was to be a stay-at-home mom. As a fulltime housewife, I was in my element. I made all our clothes including bras and panties, as well as my husband's suits, our drapes, and upholstery.

Chuck had two gardens. The girls picked the produce, and I processed it via canning, dehydrating, or freezing. We never bought processed food. I went to a co-op for eggs, butter, and milk.

One day, Chuck and I decided we were going to put a wallpaper border around the top of the wall in our master bedroom. I bought a metal ladder at a garage sale without checking to see if it had any flaws. Hardwood floors were all over the house, because we had not put in carpet yet.

Because I take after my paternal grandmother, I have fought a weight problem my entire life. On my five-foot-six-inch frame and a size fourteen, I wanted to get down to the small frame of my body. So I went to our family doctor, and he put me on diet pills. With the pills, I was not hungry. At only six hundred calories a day I went down to 137 pounds and wore a size seven dress. I was thrilled.

On a Saturday morning, I started working on the border. After I got the first piece up, I turned around to sit on the top of the ladder. Chuck brought me a cup of coffee and yelled, "Honey, don't sit on the ladder!"

I was so thrilled I could fit between the rungs of the ladder; I did not listen. After I sat down, the ladder collapsed. The back legs went one way, and the front legs went another. Unbelievably, the back legs of the ladder were broken where they should have attached to the seat.

I landed on the metal ladder on my spine at L-2, L-3, L-4, and L-5. I was in so much pain. Chuck took me to the ER where they did all kinds of tests. The doctors informed me that I had herniated the three disks. They gave us a choice. They would admit me and put me in traction for three months, or we could go home after they taught me how to put myself in traction. We chose to go home, so they gave me instructions and pain meds.

It was summer, so the girls were out of school. They were nine and ten. Every day from that day to today, I sleep with a large pillow under my legs at night or whenever I lie down. I cannot lie flat on my back.

With home traction, I lay on the floor with pillows stacked in our bedroom chair. I put my calves up on the pillows and basically hung there, with my butt not touching the ground. Chuck brought our black and white twelve-inch TV into the bedroom and set it on the floor beside me.

I lay there all day watching TV and taking pain meds. The girls would go play in the neighborhood, then come home at lunch and fix a sandwich for me, give me water, etc. Good friends in the neighborhood watched out for the girls and came to check on me.

Whenever I was not lying in traction on the floor, I had to wear a plastic back brace that was molded to my back. I wore it for standing or especially riding in the car.

That was the first injury to my back. Since the fall on the ladder, I have lived with constant pain. Even today, when I walk, I look down at the ground. I am so afraid of another fall.

Pothole Fall

In 1991, I was on our local school board, and we were hosting the Perdue Band. After the football game, around eleven o'clock, I went to school to pick up two girls who would stay overnight with us.

One of the girls, Tasha, asked me a question. In that millisecond, I turned to her as my left leg stepped into a pothole. The pothole was only two inches deep but five feet across. Down I went! I landed at the very edge of the pothole. It happened so quickly, I couldn't even brace myself. I took the full blow and landed between my upper lip and my nose, fracturing my two front teeth and a lower front tooth.

Once my teeth were fixed, I had pain and numbness in my arms and neck along with my lower back pain. For some reason, I did not equate the fall with the pain in my arms and neck.

In 2001, I went to a pain doctor in Cleveland for the numbness in my arms and the pain in my neck. The doctor did an MRI. Chuck was with me while I sat on the exam table.

When the doctor came in, he said "Well, you have five herniated disks from C-3 to C-7 in your neck." He talked more, but I never heard another word he said. I was in shock. Now I have herniated five disks in my neck and four disks in my lumbar spine.

When Chuck and I got in the car to head home, he said, "Meet me downtown tomorrow and we'll go get your neck pillow."

"What neck pillow?"

From this visit, Chuck and I realized the importance of having another set of ears when you are learning about your medical condition and care. When you are the patient, you are trying to capture everything the doctor is saying to you. Having that second set of ears is so important, through all your ages but especially as you get older.

Another Injury to my Lower Back

In 2004, we flew to Italy to attend a wedding at Lake Como. The daughter of our dear friends was getting married, and we were so thrilled to go. We started out in Vienna, because Chuck wanted to attend a concert to hear Bach and Vivaldi being played. We also saw where Bach had lived in Vienna.

Then we went to Venice for a week and loved every minute of the trip. In Venice we stayed at the Hotel Danieli, right on the water. We also toured Saint Mallow Square. After Venice we went to Lake Como for the beautiful wedding. To be in Italy and Lake Como was a dream come true.

At the reception, I left to go to the bathroom. After having my left knee replacement in 2001, I was very cautious with stairs and walking. I went up three steps, across the landing, then eight more steps up. Coming down, I held onto the rail for the eight steps. At the landing, I looked at the last three steps which had no railing.

I hesitated and said to myself, "Denece, it is only three steps." I took one step and down I went. My right knee buckled. I landed on my lower back at the edge of the concrete step.

When we got home, I went to the pain doctor. He did an MRI and told me I had herniated the L-5/S-1 disk in my back. So now my lower back has herniations from L-1 down to S-1. This also included the five disks in my neck which were pretty messed up.

Ever since the original injury in 1973, I have been determined not to get addicted to narcotic pain pills.

One day, in 2006, I was talking to Leslie on the phone. "Mom, how is your pain today?"

"Well, it was a Darvocet morning, a Vicodin afternoon, and a Percocet night."

Chronic Pain Management Program

After that conversation with Leslie, I went to my internist because I was heading down a path I did not want to go down. My internist recommended me to the Chronic Pain Management Program at the Cleveland Clinic. I started the program in September of 2006. It was a month long from 7:45 to 4:30, five days a week. We had seven counselors, a nurse assigned to us, Dr. Covington who ran the program, one-on-one counseling, group counseling, physical therapy, and Dr. Covington's assistant.

The first week of the program, Dr. Covington told us, "The pain you are in right now will be the pain level you will have the rest of your life. There is no magic pill or magic surgery that will take this away. The purpose of this program is to teach you how to live with pain without drugs."

That first week, I cried all day long. It was exceptionally hard to accept that there was no cure. At the end of the month-long program, I accepted that this was my life, and I had a choice to make every day. I could give into the pain, not get out of bed, not live a life, and be down all the time. Or I could accept that this *was* my life, choose to live an engaged life, and find joy every day.

Since then, I have lived with chronic pain every second of the day. The hardest thing for me to do each day is to just get out of bed. It is the first decision of my day. This program truly gave me my life back. I have put great determination and effort into not being addicted to narcotics.

When I started this journey in 1973 with my first injury on the ladder, I was determined not to give in to the pain. At twenty-seven I thought I would take drugs for the pain when I was past seventy. Here I am at seventy-five and I still fight hard not to take drugs.

In 2006, I finished The Chronic Pain Management Program. It really helped me put more energy into the quality of my life. Whether or not to give into pain is a choice I make every day.

These are the tools I use every day to refocus on something besides pain:

- I have a jigsaw puzzle going all the time. Usually by four o'clock my pain level is at seven or eight. The puzzle refocuses my mind away from the pain.

- I make jam. When our girls were growing up, I made homemade jam. In 2015, I decided to make jam again. I went into my kitchen, put my screaming women (Katie Perry) on Alexa, and started in.

- I wear a TENS (Transcutaneous Electrical Nerve Stimulator) unit on my lower back. I place four pads on my back, then press the TENS unit for continuous buzzing. It has helped my chronic pain so much.

- I go to sleep with the television on. Many studies say don't sleep with electronics but for me it is essential. I turn the volume down to barely audible, so that my brain will focus on the TV instead of the pain. I usually have Law and Order on because it is mostly talking and not loud noise. By doing this, I do not take narcotics for my pain.

- My pain doctor at the Cleveland Clinic created a pain cream for me to put on whichever area is hurting that day. This compound prescription has ten percent Ketamine, six percent Gabapentin, three percent

Diclofenac, two percent Baclofen, two percent Cyclobenzaprine, one percent Bupivacaine HCI.

Jam Recipe

When I started making my jam, I discovered there was a fruit market in Avon, Ohio with cherries, pitted and stemmed from Michigan. They were fresh, so I ordered ten pounds. They made the best cherry jam ever. I bought frozen three-berry fruit from Costco. The raspberry, blueberry, and blackberry combination made excellent jam.

My son-in-law, is a trained chef. We came up with pineapple, mango, ginger jam. It is his recipe and the jam that everyone wants, over and above all others.

Pineapple, Mango, Ginger Jam

One fresh pineapple cut into small pieces
One bag of frozen mango from Costco
Ginger
3 cups mango chopped up fine (I use my Vita-mix)
3 cups pineapple chopped fine (Vita-Mix)
2 heaping tsp. shaved ginger
1 cup water
3 tsp. calcium water
2 tsp. pectin

In a jam maker, combine all ingredients except the pectin, cooking for twenty-two minutes. After the pectin is put in, cook for ten minutes longer. Put into cleaned canning jars and a hot water bath for ten minutes to seal the jars. The yield is two tall pint jars, two-half pint jars and three-one quarter pint jars.

The first time I made jam, Chuck was working in the dining room. He came into the kitchen and said, "This is the first time I have seen your face with no pain on it."

I had found another way to refocus my brain from pain. The first year, I made 257 jars of jam. I gave them away to whomever came over. Our friends would bring the jars back to me so I could fill them again.

I also love to bake. I ran a cake decorating business out of my home for twelve years, putting great effort into making my cakes different that would stand out. My recipe for cakes, cupcakes, etc. follows:

Denece's Cake Recipe

Chocolate cake: Dunkin Hines Cake™ mix, and **only** Dunkin Hines cake mix. **Do not follow the directions on the box.** Use one cake mix, one package of Dream Whip™, one cup of water, one cup of Hellman's™ mayonnaise and **only** Hellman's mayonnaise. Then add four eggs instead of three. Mix and bake per package instructions.

For yellow, white, caramel, strawberry, or all other flavors, follow the directions on the box. The only thing added is the one package of Dream Whip and four eggs instead of three.

Filling the cupcakes: purchase a cutter to cut out the center of the cupcake. Push it in the center of the cupcake, twist, and pull it out. I saved the centers in a bowl because it was my husband's favorite part. Fill the cupcakes with jam that you have made or store-bought jam. Then ice the cupcakes, with my icing.

Icing: Mix two sticks of real butter (no off-brands), one stick of Crisco™ (again no off- brand). Mix these together, add your coloring and your flavors. Mix it all together. Add two pounds of confectioner's sugar. Put half the bag with the butter mixture and mix well. Add three tablespoons of water and mix well. Add the rest of the confectioner's sugar and the other three or four tablespoons of water. Mix well.

Longaberger

In 1991, I started selling Longaberger products. The Longaberger Company was an American manufacturer and distributor of handcrafted maple wood products. Dave Longaberger started the company in 1973 in the small Ohio town of Dresden.

The company offered a wide distribution of their products throughout the US. The baskets were sold through consultants who offered home shows where they invited their friends, and the consultant demonstrated the many uses for the baskets. The company eventually added pottery, wrought iron, and home décor.

I attended many home parties for the baskets and fell in love with them. I talked to Chuck about wanting to sign up as a consultant. It was the only thing in our entire marriage that he asked me not to do. He knew I would go gang busters, and he was afraid he would never see me.

One day he said, "Honey, if you really want to do this, sign up."

When I started my business, Chuck had a Mac computer. This Mac computer was so early it only had a six-inch screen. Chuck said, "Honey why don't you type in your customer base, then you can print out labels for your flyers."

"I'm afraid I'll crash your computer."

"You won't crash it, I promise."

When he came home that night, I had crashed the computer. He asked me what I had done. I had no clue how, but it happened. Later, I did learn how to use the computer and continued to grow my business, recruiting new consultants. Eventually I had seven consultants under me which moved me to become a branch manager with the company.

I held monthly branch meetings, teaching about the new products coming out, how to sell them, and how to recognize that this was a business. Chuck had taught me early on, "If you don't recognize yourself as a business, no one else will." This was not a sorority. It was a business.

As my business grew, eventually 57 consultants were under me from across the country. When I signed up a new consultant from out-of-state, I traveled to them and showed them how it was done. We did home shows or an event in their town.

I worked in my office from 7:00 am to 7:00 pm. Chuck said he never saw me not working, but I truly loved my job. I spoke three different times at the Longaberger Convention, taught how to do a home show, an open house, and how not to spend your entire paycheck on your consultants. I also did a lot of travel with my consultants.

When my body went into chronic pain in 2006, I was living with the pain every second of the day. Every morning, I woke up at a three or four pain level. One morning I woke up at pain level eight. I was losing 10 to 12 days a month to pain, with levels between eight and nine. At those levels, I could not function. That day, I realized God was telling me I needed to quit my job.

The morning God talked to me about my job, I realized being a manager of 57 consultants and living in chronic pain, was not fair to my consultants. I could not focus 100 percent of my time on their business. When any of my consultants called me about their business, I owed them my full attention. If I could not give them my full attention, it was not fair to them. My pain was affecting their business.

I called Pam at The Longaberger Company. She was vice president and someone I had worked with, so she knew me. When Pam answered my call, I started crying so hard, I could not talk.

Pam said, "Denece, what is going on?"

When I could finally talk again, I told her I needed to resign as a branch leader.

"Why?"

"Because I live with chronic pain from falls I have had since 1973. I just completed the Cleveland Clinic's Chronic Pain Management program, and I have finally realized that I am losing at least 12 days a month to chronic pain.

It is not fair to my group for me to be unavailable to them. My being unavailable really affects their business. As a leader I need to answer the phone, help them resolve a problem, or just give them encouragement."

"Denece, I am so sorry!"

Normally if a leader resigns their group, the consultants are divided up and put under other leaders in their town. The miracle was how God gave me a plan to divide up my group.

"God presented me with this idea last night. I would like to divide up my group into three groups with three new leaders for each group."

"We've never done that," Pam said.

"I realize that, but just because it has never been done, does not mean it cannot be done."

I explained to her how to do this option with a Westlake Ohio group, a Germantown Ohio group, and my out-of-state consultants who would go under a consultant in Minnesota.

I said, "If you look at the sales from my group, you will see they have consistently high sales. The groups I mentioned are a very tight group. To just divide them up and put them with leaders they don't have a working relationship with is going to affect their morale and thus affect their sales. What I am proposing *can* be done."

Pam said, "I'll have to take this to our lawyers, and I'll get back to you." She called me the next day and said, "Denece, we are going to do it the way you devised."

Relieved, I told Pam, "I will personally call each consultant and make them aware that I am retiring. I will mail to each consultant a delete letter and a new contract letter stipulating who they will be going under. They will send the two contracts back to me and I will mail all 57 sets to the company in one packet."

Normally if you resign, you must stay out of the business for six months. Doing it this way meant there was no disruption in their business. Pam agreed to my plan, so I started the process rolling.

At first, on days that my pain levels were low, I really missed everyone. But on the days, it was eight or nine, I felt no guilt on top of the pain.

Shoulder Pain

In 2015, I had rotator cuff surgery on my right shoulder. I had arthritis in both shoulders. Dr. Brems from The Cleveland Clinic did my right shoulder, and it went great. I healed, and it does not bother me. Dr. Brems retired after my right rotator cuff surgery, so I had to find a new doctor for my shoulders.

Dr. Riccehetti did my left rotator cuff shoulder surgery in 2017. The surgery did not fix the pain, so he had to do it again in 2018. Then he told me, eventually, I would need shoulder replacement. There was too much damage to my left shoulder from arthritis.

Fall Down the Stairs

In 2020, Chuck was back in the hospital to have his heart cardiovert. The doctors stopped his heart, then restarted it hopefully in rhythm.

I called my friend/sister Valerie to come up from Dayton, Ohio to Cleveland so she could help me with our dog Sydney. I wanted to stay in the hospital with Chuck. I spent four days with him in the hospital sleeping in a recliner chair. On the fifth day, I went home to sleep in my own bed. When I woke up the next morning, I could not get out of bed. Through all the years of chronic pain, I never went to the hospital for it. That day, I asked Val to call the EMT's to take me to the hospital. I was at a 10 and could not get out of bed.

They admitted me. Now Chuck was on the fourth floor, and I was on the third floor. They gave me stronger pain meds, kept me for one day, and then released both of us. Val picked us up and took us home. We went into the guest room so Chuck and I could lie in bed with Val in the recliner chair. We were watching TV and Chuck said he would like the raised toilet in our basement. He wanted the extra height of the raised toilet, because he was very weak.

Without saying a word to either of them, I got up and walked to the end of our stair rail. I could see my world going black, so I put both hands on the rail, assuming I would fall on the carpeted floor. Valerie watched me pass out and flip over the rail, do two somersaults, three flip flops back and forth, and land on the hard wood floor. I had fallen 14 steps.

When I woke up, I was on the last step of the stairs, looking down at myself lying on the hardwood floor. On my right side, lying in a fetal position with my left arm lying on a box. My legs were curled under me.

As I looked at my body, I vividly remember thinking, *Huh, that's me.* I heard myself talking to God, going back and forth with, "Is this my time to die or not?"

His voice is all-encompassing around my brain and my body. It feels like I am safe and cared for by our Lord. I can still vividly remember feeling my soul reentering my body. I felt this big 'swish,' and I was back lying on the hardwood floor. That was the last thing I remember. No memory of the EMT's putting me on the gurney and taking me to the hospital. I was in the hospital for five days. Leslie came from Michigan and stayed with me during the daytime.

I asked Leslie, "Did I talk with people? Was I aware of the room and you being with me?"

"Yes, you talked to the nurses, doctors, and the staff."

There is a strange feeling around not remembering that is hard to describe. I lost five days of my life and cannot remember anything. Those five days are a void in my memory that have never come back.

From the fall, I fractured my sternum and the T-6 vertebra in my back. After five days, they moved me to rehabilitation at Rae Ann Rehab in Westlake, Ohio. The first memory I have of this fall was when I was in a Hoyer™ (patient) lift as they were transferring me from the ambulance gurney into a bed. I was screaming at the top of my lungs.

Mary Jane, one of the physical therapists, took a pillow, doubled it in half, wrapped it with packing tape, and handed it to me. Whenever they moved me, I would hug "Mary Jane" my pillow, so it would not hurt as bad.

I was in rehab for six weeks. While I was healing, Leslie and my dear friend Nancy came to see me and be with Chuck. They helped Chuck order a lift chair to be put in for our stairs and arrange a hospital bed for when I came home. They also needed to have a rough talk with Chuck.

Leslie told Chuck that my fall down the stairs was his fault for not taking better care of himself. She told her father that I did too much for him and that I did not think of myself. By not paying attention to his body and his two heart conditions, he was putting me at risk as well as himself. His decisions impacted the entire family.

When I fell down my 14 stairs at home, I fractured the T-6 vertebra in my back and my sternum. The sternum healed just fine, but the T-6 fracture is always with me. So now I have five herniated disks in my neck, the T-6 fracture, and herniations from L-1 to S-1.

The pain from this fracture was much higher than a ten. Here's how the pain levels are recognized:

Zero: No Pain — comfortable.

One: Minimal — pain is hardly noticeable.

Two: Mild — a low level of pain. I am aware of my pain only when I pay attention to it.

Three: Uncomfortable — my pain bothers me, but I can ignore it most of the time.

Four: Moderate — I am constantly aware of my pain, but I can continue some functions.

Five: Distracting — I am constantly aware of my pain. I cannot do some of the activities I need to do each day because of the pain.

Six: Distressing — I think about my pain all the time. I give up most activities because of my pain.

Seven: Unmanageable — I am in pain all the time. It keeps me from doing anything.

Eight: Intense — my pain is so severe that it is hard to think of anything else. Talking and listening are very difficult.

Nine: Severe — my pain is all I can think about. I can barely talk or move because of the pain. I cannot think clearly.

Ten: I am in bed and cannot move due to my pain. I need someone to take me to the hospital to get help with my pain.

The medical community will tell you it only goes from 0-10 but since 2006 when my body went into chronic pain, I have said that 10 is not the top number. When I'm at a 10, I can only scream, definitely not talk. I wanted to scream at them, "You live with my pain levels and tell me it only goes to a 10!"

Back in rehab, every time they had to move me, I hugged my pillow, which I now called Mary Jane. They had to do everything for me: bathe me, clean me up, and reposition me in my bed. The staff at Rae Ann Westlake Rehab facility were wonderful. I had physical therapy, occupational therapy, and memory work for the concussion I received from the fall. The therapies were every day, sometimes twice a day, whether I wanted to or not.

During the first two weeks in rehab, I could not see my life going forward. You know how you wake up in the morning and you plan your day? "I'm going to sew today, bake today, clean house today, go to the grocery store, etc." I could not see life going forward. It was very frightening.

I asked God, "Why am I still here? What do You have planned for me?" I talked to God a lot. The message he gave me was that I still had a lot to do in this life. God had been telling me for seven years that I was going to write this book about the miracles in my life.

I always answered God back, "I'm not a writer, I have no training in writing a book." Little did I know that seven years later, I would write this book. God was right.

After six weeks in rehab, I came home. I slept in a rented hospital bed in our family room. Because of the T-6 fracture, they did not want me to bend over or pick anything up. I moved very cautiously in the bed and let my body heal. An aide stayed with me at night, because I was petrified of falling. If I had to go downstairs, someone needed to be behind me so I could go down backwards.

Epidural Bleed

Since the T-6 fracture, my pain levels have increased significantly. It has been the tipping point in my chronic pain. I was getting epidural injections in my neck, lower back and now especially T-6. The shots would give me pain relief for about six months.

In June of 2023, I had an injection in the T-6 vertebrae just like many other times. An hour after getting the injection, I was back in my apartment when my entire back went into an excruciating spasm. I was screaming at the top of my lungs.

My daughter, Laura, called the EMT's. They took me out of Riley Crossing on a gurney. I was screaming the whole time. I am a very hard stick for an IV, because my veins are tiny. They don't roll or collapse but are just hard to get a needle into. So I screamed for four hours.

When they finally got an IV going and could give me pain meds, I stopped screaming. They did an MRI of my spine and discovered I had developed an epidural bleed from T-3 to T-10. This type of bleeding happens in one in 100,000 injections. The doctors were trying to decide if I needed surgery to open my back to extract the blood. They admitted me to the hospital on the Neuro-ICU floor in case the surgery was going to move forward. The blessing or "miracle" here is that I did not have to have the surgery.

When I came home from the hospital, I was not allowed to lift more than five pounds, pull, tug, sew, or write my book. Basically, I had to go home and let my back heal from the blood. The hope was that the blood would be reabsorbed back into my body. The doctors told me it could be as much as four months for the blood to reabsorb.

For four weeks I was very careful. On week five I decided I would sew just for twenty minutes. They did not want me bent over a sewing machine or at the computer. In my infinite wisdom, I also decided to go pull four weeds in my back yard. Well, for the next two days my back flared up in pain. For two days I was at a pain level of an eight.

Because of my chronic pain, I keep the volume on my bedroom TV turned down low. My brain will concentrate on the TV conversation and not on the pain. Pulling together all my tools to refocus was not working.

Suddenly, my TV went black. I kept waiting for the show to come back on. Ten minutes passed and it was still black. Then a picture of Jesus in an oval frame appeared on my screen. Jesus was looking up at heaven. After those 10 minutes, I decided maybe Jesus was trying to tell me something.

I closed my eyes and prayed. "Jesus, is the message you are giving me that there are only one set of feet in the sand and they're not mine? Are you carrying me?" When I opened my eyes, the picture was still there, but my pain was gone completely. Since then, my pain has been normal and functional.

I shared this story and the picture of Jesus in my TV with my friend, Bonnie Smith. This picture is framed in the living room of a resident here at Riley Crossing. Bonnie had taken a picture of the painting and was trying to transfer the picture to her TV so she could say the rosary to it. She could not get it to show up on her TV. Instead, it showed up on *my* TV. The picture came at the exact moment I needed it. This was a miracle.

You may wonder why I consider chronic pain a miracle, but it has enhanced my life. Would I like to have no chronic pain? Of course, but it has made me appreciate the life I live. The gift it has given me is that I look at life through a different lens. When my pain levels are low, I enjoy my life and give back to people through sewing, canning, and baking. When my levels are high, I have tools to refocus my brain, so I am not so overwhelmed with the pain.

MIRACLES

With the original back injury, I could do traction at home.

Chronic Pain Management gave me my life back.

The miracle that I survived falling 14 steps. So many things could have happened. I could have died, been paralyzed from the neck down, broken numerous bones in my body.

With the epidural bleed, no surgery was needed to open my back up and get the blood out. It dissolved on its own.

Jesus showed up in my TV.

For 50 years, not one of the herniated disks has ruptured.

GI BLEED

In 2006, when my body went into chronic pain, Chuck and I started sleeping in different rooms. This was a huge loss for both of us, but it was necessary. I had to fall asleep with the television on and turned down low, so I could go to sleep. At night, my brain would focus on the television show and not on how much pain I was in. Chuck could not sleep with electronics on.

In 2015, in the middle of the night, I got out of my bed to go to the bathroom. As I made my way to the toilet, I felt all this stuff running down my legs and feet. I was not awake enough to have the presence of mind to turn on a light and no clue what was running down my legs. When I sat on the toilet to urinate, I swished on the toilet seat. I was having a great deal of trouble not falling off the toilet. In my head, I was trying to figure out what was going on.

I opened my eyes enough to see this extremely bright light. Where was it coming from? Then I heard God's voice very clearly, "If you do not get off this toilet, you are going to die."

I was barely awake when He said it again, "If you do not get off this toilet, you are going to die."

I got up and stumbled my way into the master bedroom and pounded on Chuck to wake up. He seemed confused, then looked at me — horrified. I had blood all over me. I was incoherent. He walked me back to my walk-in bathtub and helped me sit down. Chuck took my bloody night gown off and called the EMT's.

When they came, the EMT assessed me. At one point I remember thinking, "I'm butt naked in this tub and a strange man is looking at me." Then I passed out and was not aware of anything. I do remember them draping a sheet over my naked body as they put me in a chair to take me down the stairs. I do not remember the ambulance ride, the time in the ER, or being moved to a room.

When I woke up in my room, the hospital staff had cleaned me up and put me in a hospital gown. Chuck was sitting by me, so I asked him what happened. He told me about the house, the emergency room, and ending up in this room.

They had me on a cardiac ward. All I could think of was *Oh my gosh! I'm on a cardiac ward. My dad died at sixty-four and here I am at sixty-four on a cardiac floor! I must be dying.*

The doctor came in and told me I had had a gastro-intestinal bleed. They did two colonoscopies to make sure it was nothing else. They determined the bleed was from the NSAID's (non-steroidal anti-inflammatory drugs) I took for my chronic pain.

It took six days for the bleed to stop so I could go home. I have never taken an NSAID again.

MIRACLE

The Miracle was God shining the light, waking me up and telling me to get off the toilet so I didn't bleed to death.

AUSTRALIA

After Chuck retired, he wanted to travel the world, specifically to France and Australia. With his diagnosis of congestive heart failure and atrial fibrillation, I was nervous to even *think* about us traveling.

In 2018, I gave in to our going to France. Chuck planned the entire trip. We spent a month touring Normandy Beach. We stayed with a couple in their bed and breakfast. The art pieces around their home were things they salvaged from the water off the beach. These items were leftovers from the D-Day invasion. They had a propeller blade from one of the German planes.

Chuck's dad made four D-Day landings during WWII. He missed Normandy because he had to have his appendix out. It was amazing to walk Normandy Beach. A number of the landing boats are still on the beach, 70 years after the invasion. We brought back a flask from Normandy. Next, we did a Viking cruise. Monte Carlo, and lastly Paris. We had a fabulous time.

In 2019, we decided we could do Australia. Because of the long trip, we traveled first class. With my back, I needed to be able to lie down and stretch out. With Chuck's lungs and heart issues, he needed the non-stress. The trip Chuck planned included Sydney for six days, Cairns for a week, and on to New Zealand for a two-week cruise.

We arrived in Sydney. As people were deboarding the plane, I got nauseous. I went into the bathroom and threw up several times. When I got back to my seat, they put me on oxygen and called the EMT's to assess me.

I went to the doctor in the airport. He gave me meds for the nausea, and we went on to our hotel. In our room, Chuck went right to sleep. I was up all night, feeling worse and worse. When Chuck woke up, I asked him to call the EMT's again. I felt like I was having heart problems. The EMT's took me to the hospital where they did a complete work-up for my heart. Everything came out good. But they told me to stay down and let my body adjust to the new location.

We did not get to see anything of Sydney. Three days later we flew to Cairns. As we planned our trip, we knew that Chuck would be on oxygen, especially for the flights. We thought we had everything taken care of for his oxygen, but we were wrong. The airlines had approved his oxygen for the flight to Australia and the flight home. When we got to the airport for our flight to Cairns, we boarded the plane and sat in our seats for an hour. No one knew what was holding up the flight.

The flight attendant came and asked us to leave the plane. We were confused. Apologizing to everyone, we got off the plane. The plane took off without us.

We discovered Chuck's oxygen had not been approved for us to fly in Australia. We went to a hotel as the airlines worked to get his oxygen approved. Once everything was approved, we went back to the airport. The flight went great. We were flying from the southern part of Sydney, Australia to the northern part of Cairn, Australia.

When we landed, we were so tired. We ate dinner and then went to bed. The next morning, Chuck woke me up, and said, "You have to take me to the ER." He was bleeding from his rectum. This had never happened to him before.

At the ER, they did some tests and discovered Chuck had a hemorrhoid that had burst, thus causing the bleeding. He was fine so we went back to the hotel.

That night Chuck slept great, but I started getting sicker and sicker. When he got up, I told him, "This time you have to call the EMT's for me."

Back at the ER, they took me to a room. I lay there for seven hours, coughing into a blanket. I was so worried about Chuck because he was sitting only three feet from me. Finally, they admitted me to a room. We discovered I had Influenza A. I was quarantined in isolation so Chuck could not be in the same room with me. He did venture out to see parts of Cairns.

While I was sick with the flu, I called our girls, crying, "One of you has to fly over here to help us get home." I felt like if they did not get us, I would be coming home in a body bag. I was that sick for six days. Laura flew over to help get us home.

When the nurses were moving me to another room, I had two grand mal seizures. I had never had a seizure before. After the seizures I developed PRES (posterior reversible encephalopathy syndrome) of the brain. Symptoms of PRES are seizures, disturbed vision, headache, and altered mental state. The doctors thought I developed this because my blood pressure medicine had not been taken accurately. We took in my medications but did not have an accurate list of when to take them. I was in the hospital for six days in the intensive care unit.

The doctors told us I had to stay in Cairns for two weeks so my vitals could be monitored. Because Laura was a doctor, they let her take my vitals instead of us having go back and forth to the hospital.

Laura and Chuck went sightseeing around Cairns. The only outing I did was to the Koala sanctuary. I have pictures of me holding a koala with a parrot on my shoulder.

After seven days, with my vitals finally stable, they released me to fly. We flew from Cairns to Brisbane, spent the night, then from Brisbane to Los Angeles. When we landed in the United States, I wanted to kiss the ground. I was so happy to be back in the States. We spent the night, and the next day flew to Cleveland. Laura spent the night, and the next day flew home to Minneapolis.

Once we were home, our doctors at The Cleveland Clinic checked me out. My heart was fine, but because of the seizures and the PRES, I must be on Keppra for the rest of my life.

MIRACLE

The Miracle is that I did not die, and I have no side effects from the PRES.

THE MERKABAH

Chuck was a deeply spiritual man. While he was raised in the Presbyterian Church, he explored many different religions and spiritual traditions. In 1973, Chuck studied meditation. He became enthralled with TM (Transcendental Meditation), a form of silent mantra meditation that promotes relaxed awareness, stress relief, self-development, and higher states of consciousness.

Chuck had been searching for a method to provide balance and calm in his life. We started a meditation practice together, meditating twice a day. TM meditation became a lifelong practice for him. As for me, I practiced it for about three years but had a hard time calming my mind down and would often sleep. Our girls thought that was funny to see Mom sleeping and Dad meditating.

Chuck had a vibrant spiritual practice his whole life and felt a strong connection to God. He had many spiritual friends and teachers over the years. One of those close family friends was Jen Maitreya, Leslie's best friend of 30 years. Leslie and Jen would often visit Chuck and me when she flew in from Massachusetts. We would cook together and have a wonderful time.

In July 2020, about three months before Chuck passed away, Jen and Leslie visited. Jen shared a spiritual practice she had taken up, using the Merkabah. She showed us a beautiful pendant in the form of a three-dimensional star on a short silver chain. Here's a description of the Merkabah:

"The Merkabah, also known as the Star Tetrahedron, is a sacred geometry symbol formed by combining two opposing tetrahedrons to form a three-dimensional star shape. It is a Hebrew word with ancient Egyptian origins that means **chariot**. However, it is made up of three separate components, which phonetically means light, body, and spirit and can offer protection to the user, aligning them more fully with their higher self. It can be visualized as a spinning star tetrahedron around the body, using meditation techniques to activate the Merkabah energies." (The Transcendent Geometry of the Merkaba)

Chuck was fascinated with Jen's pendant and said he would love to have one. When Jen returned home, she went to the local store where she had bought hers and purchased the same one for Chuck. She mailed it to Chuck. He was thrilled. They had several conversations about it, and he told her he often kept it in his pants pocket.

The miracle occurred after Chuck passed. While we were at the hospital Leslie remembered how he kept the Merkabah in his pocket. She searched his pockets, but it was not there. When we got home, she searched all over the house and could not find it anywhere. Leslie wanted to find it to remember her dad, because she knew how much it meant to him.

Several days passed with much activity planning Chuck's funeral. Afterwards, the girls had to go back to their homes. But they traveled back to Cleveland each month to help me go through our things and get the house ready to sell. During each visit, we all looked for the Merkabah. No luck.

One visit in February, the girls were in Chuck's office going through his things. Leslie was sad that she had not found the Merkabah. She came down to the kitchen to take a break. When she went back into his office, she was shocked to look down at an open box she had passed many times. Nothing was in the box before, but now Chuck's Merkabah pendant was lying in the empty box.

Leslie screamed and showed us the pendant. She was overjoyed and we knew Chuck was right there with us. To this day, Leslie keeps her dad's Merkabah with her.

MIRACLE

Leslie called Jen to tell her about the miracle of finding Chuck's Merkabah.

MY GRANDCHILDREN'S QUILTS

After Chuck and I married, we got pregnant with Leslie the first three weeks into the marriage. We were so shocked and thrilled at the same time. We were using birth control, but when God decides you are going to have a child, you *are going* to have the child.

Chuck and I were living in Houston and had moved into our first apartment. When my parents found out that I was pregnant, they drove over to Houston from San Antonio. Mother told me, "Come on, we're going shopping."

I thought we were going to buy baby clothes but no — she bought me a sewing machine. I had taken home economics in school, so I knew how to sew but did not have a machine.

At Sears, Mother bought me a $100 portable sewing machine. In 1967, this was an expensive machine. We went to the fabric store and bought baby clothes' patterns and fabric. I started making Leslie's clothes.

When we got pregnant with Laura, Leslie was only five months old. Again, we were using birth control, but God decided we were having another baby. We were shocked but also excited. The girls would be only fourteen months apart. They would grow up like twins.

When I was seven months along with Laura, Chuck's company Armco Steel, moved us to the corporate office in Middletown, Ohio. We had never lived outside the state of Texas. This move was exciting but also a little bit scary for me. Chuck was excited to start a new path in his career. I would not be close to my parents or his parents. They could no longer just drive over. We were on our own.

We moved into a townhome with two bedrooms, two baths, a living room and kitchen. We also had a patio. We moved in the month of July, and Laura was born in August. When we had our first snowfall, we went outside to take pictures. I wore a linen dress, because I did not own a pair of jeans. The picture shows me holding baby Laura and holding Leslie's hand in a foot of snow.

My new sewing machine was put to good use. I took every sewing class possible. First, I made the girls' clothes and my clothes. I found a new sewing instructor and she taught me how to make Chuck's suits, my nightgowns, my underwear, and his pajamas. After four years of sewing on my Singer machine, I told Chuck I had worn the machine out and needed a new one. He did not believe me.

Chuck traveled with Armco to many out-of-town events. He was in the building technologies division. He was going to California to man a booth at the National School Board Convention. They were demonstrating the use of metal buildings in school districts. I had the privilege of going with him. Chuck packed the slacks that I had made him for the trip.

He was in his booth, so I walked around the exhibit area. I settled into the sewing display area looking at the new machines. In 1969, Home Economics was still taught in schools.

Chuck found me and said, "Honey, come on. We need to go upstairs."

In our room, he showed me where the crotch of his slacks had come out. I reminded him, "I've been telling you my machine is worn out."

He changed clothes and said, "Go down to the convention and pick out whatever kind of machine you want."

I was so excited. My friends said I did it on purpose with his slacks, but I would never have done that to Chuck.

We built our first home in Germantown which was about a 20-minute drive for Chuck's work. When we got home, I bought a new Elna machine. I continued sewing classes and was really in my element. Sewing was where I felt centered, where I found myself.

I discovered a new school where I could take sewing lessons. At the Joint Vocational School, I learned how to make drapes and upholster furniture. I went to garage sales and bought used furniture, then reupholstered it. I made all the drapes in our new house.

As the girls grew up, I still made all their clothes. When Leslie started junior high, she said, "Mom, I don't want you to make my clothes anymore." She wanted to shop retail like her friends. I told her, "Fine, but you'll have less clothes than Laura. I have a budget for both of you, so Laura will have more clothes." Leslie was fine with that.

This plan went along fine for about six months. One day Leslie came home from school and wanted these light lavender Calvin Klein jeans. They would cost about four months of her clothing budget.

The next day, I went down to my fabric store where I shopped at least once a week. As God would have it, I found the light lavender denim on the flat fold table with the Calvin Klein name on the selvage of the fabric.

A flat fold comes from designers. When they cut out a pattern for a design, they do 10 layers of the fabric, then cut at one time. If they cannot make 10 layers, it becomes a flat fold and goes to fabric stores to be purchased by the yard. I also looked in the Vogue pattern book. There it was — the Calvin Klein pattern for jeans.

When I picked the girls up from school, I told them we were going to the fabric store. They both rolled their eyes because that was the last place they wanted to go. They always felt like I took too long.

I took Leslie to see the Calvin Klein light lavender denim jeans fabric. Then I took her over to the pattern books and showed her the Vogue pattern for the Calvin Klein jeans. "If I make these jeans with the Calvin Klein denim fabric, will you wear them?"

"Yes!"

As I was making the jeans, I went to Goodwill to see if I could find anything made by Calvin Klein. As luck (or miracle) would have it, I found a blouse made by Calvin Klein with the tag in it. I bought the blouse, cut out the tag, and sewed it onto her new light lavender jeans.

When Leslie came home from school that day, she put on the new jeans. They fit perfectly. She wore them to school the next day. When she came home, she said, "Mom, you can make me anything you want." Her friends were so envious that she had a mom that could sew.

When Leslie got engaged to her first husband, I made her wedding dress. She is the only bride I have ever heard of that took out a year's subscription to Bride's Magazine. She would send me designs from wedding books and say, "I want this collar, this sleeve, this train, this veil." All while she was finishing up her senior year in college.

The dress was pretty much done when she sent me one last picture. She wanted some "windows" in her train. Windows in the satin fabric is accomplished by sewing in lace and cutting out the fabric underneath. I put the windows in, then took the dress on the dress form to a friend's house.

"Leslie, the dress is done. No more additions."

As the years went on, I continued to take any class in sewing that I could find. I even learned how to make my own bras and panties. Since I learned how to make panties, I have made my own underwear. I have not bought underwear in 40 years.

The one type of sewing I said I would *never* do was quilting. I always told Chuck if I learned how to quilt and fell in love with it, he would have to add another room onto the house just for my quilting.

When Leslie and George had our first grandchild, Kel, I woke up one morning with God telling me, "You are going to make a quilt for Kel."

I have since learned to not use the *never* word. If I say never, I might as well put a day on the calendar when I am going to do it. Instead, I have learned to say, "I don't plan on doing that. Anything but "never."

That morning, I called Leslie and said, "I'm coming over for a quick trip." Leslie lived about two and a half hours from us in Westlake. I knew they were saving Kel's clothes for their next baby or for Laura's baby.

When I got to Michigan, I asked Leslie and George for twenty of Kel's old clothes. There was one outfit that I really wanted, but George would not let me have it. It was the outfit Kel came home from the hospital in. He did not want it cut up. He wanted the memory of how tiny she was when she was born. As we were picking out the outfits, I specifically wanted ones that were meaningful to them, clothes from grandparents, aunts, close friends, etc.

When I finished the quilt, Chuck and I took it to them. I thought this would be a great blanket on the floor for Kel to play on. The blanket has *never* touched the floor. It is too precious to them.

When Laura and Rob adopted their little girl Ellabei from China, I was looking forward to making her baby quilt. She is now fourteen and her quilt is almost done. We keep finding outfits we want in the quilt.

Since that time, in 2002, I have made 30 quilts. I give them as baby gifts and ask the parents to please let their friends and relatives know about the quilt-in-process, so they can buy something special for it.

MIRACLE

God telling me I was going to do something I thought I would never do — make baby quilts.

P.E.O.

Beverly died in March of 1996. In June of '96, I held a breast cancer luncheon in my new family room. I had been living in Westlake, Ohio for almost a year. Because I was traveling to Texas each month, I hardly knew anyone.

I joined New Westside's, a club for new women who moved to the west side of Cleveland. I asked the only women I knew in Cleveland to the luncheon at my home. They invited as many people as they wanted to attend. We ended up with 40 women in my family room. I called the American Cancer Society for a guest speaker, and they sent me Karen Remine. I told Bev's story, then Karen spoke about the American Cancer Society.

After the first luncheon, Karen called and told me that she and her husband Steve would help me any way they could to spread the word about cancer. Steve was head of the Oncology unit at Fairview Hospital.

During the next four years, the luncheon was held at the Holiday Inn in Westlake. My friends from the New Westsider's club filled tables with guests each year. We grew from 40 women to over 200.

One of my friends, Bonnie Wilson and the guests at her table, came up to me after the first luncheon at the Holiday Inn. Her friends kept saying to Bonnie, "She is such a P.E.O."

I had no clue what they were talking about. Bonnie said to them, "Not yet, she needs to heal."

The next year, after the luncheon, Bonnie said to me, "Now it's time." She told me about a women's organization called P.E.O. which is a national organization about women helping women. P.E.O. stands for Philanthropic Educational Organization, one of the pioneer societies for women. It was founded on January 21, 1869, by seven students at Iowa Wesleyan College in Mount Pleasant, Iowa. Originally a small campus friendship society, P.E.O. soon blossomed to include women off campus.

Today, P.E.O. has grown from that tiny membership of seven to almost a quarter of a million members in Chapters in the United States and Canada. The P.E.O. sisterhood is passionate about its mission: promoting educational opportunities for women. Our sisterhood proudly makes a difference in women's lives with six philanthropies that include ownership of Cottey College, a women's college with two-year and four-year degree programs, and five other philanthropies that provide higher education assistance:

>P.E.O. Educational Loan Fund
>P.E.O. International Peace Scholarship Fund
>P.E.O. Program for Continuing Education
>P.E.O. Scholar Awards
>P.E.O. STAR Scholarship

P.E.O. Mission Statement

P.E.O. is a philanthropic organization where women **celebrate** the advancement of women; **educate women** through scholarships, grants, awards, loans, and stewardship of Cottey College, and **motivate** women to achieve their highest aspirations.

MIRACLE

I joined P.E.O. in 1999 and feel it was a true miracle in my life. Here was an organization that carried all the values and purpose I first learned in Rainbow Girls. It truly gave me everything I was looking for in my life.

SYDNEY'S WINGS

Sydney was the last dog for our family. Chuck and I adopted her in 2010. In September of 2023, I had to put her down because of liver failure. Sydney was my last tangible connection to our life in Westlake, Ohio.

After going to the vet on a Friday, I made the decision to put her down and not let her suffer. The test results from her blood work showed that her liver was shutting down. Sydney was dying. The vet and I scheduled to put her down on Friday of that week. Laura and Ellabei could be with me, and we could do it in my apartment — Sydney's home.

Wednesday morning, I had a vision of Chuck down on one knee with his arms open wide, waiting to accept Sydney into heaven. Chuck now has all our beagles together. Someday I will join that pack and be with them all in heaven.

The Wednesday before, I happened to look in a small star-shaped jewelry box my P.E.O. chapter had given me when I moved to Minnesota. I knew only earrings were in the box.

But something made me look in the box. When I opened the lid, I found silver wings. I have no clue where the wings came from. I asked my girls if they had given them to me, and they said, "No." I asked my friends if they had given them to me. They also said, "No."

The wings are beautiful. Chuck's name is on the back of the wings, along with the date he passed away.

I wear a cross necklace Chuck gave me for our 50th wedding anniversary. It is made of diamonds from a bracelet that Ken Altvater gave me. Ken was Chuck's best friend from high school and college roommate.

When Ken and I met for the first time, we hit it off immediately. He became more than a brother to me. We were soulmates. Ken was also Leslie's godfather.

In the late seventies, we were in Houston. Ken and I went to a jewelry store that was going out of business. Tennis bracelets had just become popular. Ken bought one with 100 diamonds in it. I wanted a bracelet so badly, but we did not have the money.

From that point on, Ken would always tell me, "When I die, this bracelet is yours." I always responded, "I want the bracelet but mostly I want *you*."

In 2008, I was working in my office and received a call from Janet, Ken's sister. She told me they had found Ken dead in his kitchen. I crumbled and sobbed on the floor in my office and called Chuck. He came home and we booked our flight to Houston.

On the flight, as I was talking to God, I realized I needed to write Ken's eulogy. People needed to know who this man was — not just a successful businessman, but who he was as a person.

One year after Ken's death, his sister, Janet came to Ohio to give me the bracelet. Janet said, "Ken wore this bracelet all the time, and he would want you to wear it all the time."

I wore it when we went out but not all the time. So on our 50th wedding anniversary, Chuck took the bracelet to our jeweler. He took 10 of the diamonds out of the bracelet and made a cross for me. Now Ken, in the diamond cross and Chuck in his wings, are with me all the time. I never take the cross or the wings off.

MIRACLES

Having a vision of Chuck on one knee waiting to accept Sydney.

Finding the wings to wear with my cross.

RILEY CROSSING

After I fell down the stairs in July of 2020, I needed someone with me. When Chuck passed away in October of 2020, my world was tossed upside down. I was still unstable and emotionally a wreck. My friend/sister Valerie Flynn and our friend Gail Burden changed their lives to come up and stay with me. I was so grateful and considered it a *miracle* that they could just stop their lives to be with me.

My girls and I decided that I needed to sell my big house and move to be close to Laura in Minnesota. I agreed with them that was what needed to be done, but I did not even know where to start. Many people believe and will tell you, after a loss, do not do anything for a year. In principle I agreed with them, but after the fall down the stairs, I really did not have that option. The house was too big for me to maintain by myself, and my girls could not give up their lives and move in with me.

At the end of October, Val and Gail moved in.

The first Thanksgiving after losing Chuck, I went to Leslie's in Michigan. They lived two and a half hours from me in Westlake. I only stayed a day, and I wanted to go home. Home, of course, was going back to be with Chuck and he was not there.

That Christmas, I flew out to Minnesota to spend the holidays with Laura's family. While I was there, Laura and I started looking for Senior Living facilities. We looked at a Senior Living place in Chaska, but it was only for Independent Living. When I eventually need to go into Assisted Living, I would have to move.

The next place we looked was Riley Crossing in Chanhassen, MN. It is nine miles to Chaska, so a perfect distance to my family. Shelley Brady showed me an apartment on the first floor. It was two bedrooms, a den for my office, two and a half baths, living room and kitchen. It has a washer and dryer in the main bathroom. I fell in love with the apartment. It is 1375 square feet. Coming from a 3400 square foot home it was quite a downsize, but it would fit me nicely.

My apartment is on the ground floor. It is the largest floor plan that Riley Crossing offers. There are only four apartments this size. We stack on top of each other. When Shelley showed me the place, I fell in love with it and could see myself living the rest of my life there. I have a patio outside the sliding glass door with mulch and plants. From day one when I looked at it, I asked if I could fence in the area outside of the patio. I told them I would pay for the fence; it would be aesthetically pleasing to the building, and it would encompass just the mulch area. The grass area would not be disrupted so the mowing of the grounds around my apartment would be clear.

I also asked if I could put in a Safe Step walk-in tub. Chuck had put one in our Westlake home, and I wanted one in my apartment. With my chronic pain my walk-in tub is a God Send. It makes my life so much easier and with less pain when I can surge hot water around my back.

Riley Crossing agreed with both of my requests, so I wrote a check for the deposit and felt I had found my new home.

The staff at Riley Crossing are so wonderful. They are all so supportive of our needs. Taryn Bartz is Executive Director. She has a hard job, I think. She is managing the seniors, their families, the staff, corporate office, and the government rules. She does an excellent job.

Shelley Brady is the Director of Sales and Outreach. She is selling our facility to new residents. She takes them on tours and explains all that Riley Crossing has to offer. Sometimes she lets me interject and sell our wonderful residence to possible new residents. I tell them about Resident Bingo and Resident Cocktail hour.

Here, I have also found my latest support group. When I had to leave Westlake, I gave up my Church, my P.E.O. Chapter and all my friends. Chuck and I lived in Ohio for 50 years. Besides grieving my Chuck, I am grieving the only life I have ever known. It was an extremely difficult decision to make but I knew I could not live in our home with just Sydney (my dog) and me. Finding Riley Crossing and settling into my new life has made my life much better. Laura and her family are only nine miles away in Chaska.

The friends I have made here are wonderful. We really support each other and have fun together. We all put effort into making Riley Crossing our home, family.

Thursday is "Church" called "The Gathering." We come from all denominations and join to worship our Lord. We also have other church services here and some people, if they have transportation, leave, and go out to their home church.

Ali Ashton and Lynn Voss are our Activity Directors and do an amazing job. We have Ladies Luncheons where we go out to restaurants in the area, we celebrate monthly birthdays and Ali and Lynn have activities for us all the time. Thursday is Riley Crossing sponsored Bingo. I am so amazed that I look forward to Bingo! If you had told me that in Westlake, I would have laughed at you. But it is just being with friends and us doing an activity together. For the month of October, we play GHOST bingo. Instead of saying "bingo" you say "Boo." November, we play GOBBLE bingo and have to say "Gobble, gobble." Christmas is GIFTS bingo, and you say, "Mine or Please." Getting everyone to laugh is such a joy and bonds all of us together like a family.

We have the Riley Crossing cocktail party on Fridays at 3:00pm and they serve wine and a special drink each week. Sometimes we have live music. We had some couples get up and dance. It is a terrific time for us to socialize and enjoy each other's company.

Every other month we have a special dinner, it can be an elegant dinner for Christmas, a bar-b-que in the summer outside, a costume party for Halloween and this year we celebrated the five-year anniversary for Riley Crossing. The party was for residents, employees, and their families. We had live music, great food, a bouncy house for the children and door prizes. They also had prizes for the five-year employees and residents that have lived here five years. One of my favorite parties was Halloween when the executive staff dressed in costumes from the Wizard of Oz.

Activities also let me organize the Resident Bingo on Saturdays. I am the Bingo bag lady! I tell everyone that if they are going to give something to

Goodwill, give it to me instead. Your trash is someone else's treasure. Everyone adores it. We have about twenty-five to thirty guests attending.

I also organized the Resident Cocktail party Saturday's at 4:00 pm. Everyone brings something to share with the group. We have wine, alcohol, and snacks to share. We have all gotten to know people we might not have gotten to know. It is especially wonderful for new residents moving into Riley Crossing. I love watching new couples getting to know other couples.

Both activities on Saturday give us something to do besides just staying in our apartment. It helps to build our foundation of friends and family. The staff and residents put effort into our being a family, where we look out for each other.

We are not allowed to give Christmas gifts to the employees. So, this year two residents and I organized cookie trays to give to every employee. We all wanted to thank the employees for taking such loving care of us. So, I asked each resident to make four dozen cookies or donate five dollars per person to purchase cookies, trays, and the cover for the trays. We started this project in September and finalized it December 10th. We made sixty-seven trays with three dozen cookies on each tray for a total of 2,444 cookies!

Another great advantage of living at Riley Crossing is the day care that is on sight. Susan is the director and does a terrific job running the program. One of the things that I missed was being around young children. The day care goes from babies to five-year-olds. On Tuesday's you can sign up to go rock the babies. I tried, but I cannot do it because of my back. At Halloween, it was so much fun to see the little children dressed in their costumes.

Jennifer is head of the Nursing Department. She has a daughter, Maddy, that is in the daycare. Last year, Maddy came running into the dining room at breakfast to give us hugs. Her hugs in the morning really start my day out right. She is a miracle and a blessing in my life.

A special miracle happened for me this year on Halloween. I was at a pain level of a ten and just miserable. I decided to go down for lunch and try to refocus my mind. I heard this laughter and figured it was a family being together. At first, I thought, I do not want to intrude. But then I decided to get up and see what all the laughter was about. One of the residents, Marlene, had her family here. Marlene's great granddaughter, Blake, was dressed in her Halloween costume. She was dressed as an "old" woman. She had a wig on, spectacle glasses, a granny dress with two strands of beads and was using a blow-up walker. The walker even had tennis balls on the back, like the ones we use here. Blake saw me and came running for me to pick her up. I could not pick her up because of my back, but I thought, "I have candy for bingo in my cart." So, I took Blake over to the candy and opened the bag for her to choose what she wanted. She was so precious; she squatted down in front of the candy and gave great thought to what she wanted. She picked up a box of M&M's and was thrilled.

Watching Blake and laughing with joy with her, made my pain stop for the rest of the day. It was another miracle for me.

MIRACLES

Finding Riley Crossing has been a Miracle for me. I could not believe I found a place that was so perfect for me.

The miracle was God giving me the idea of putting together cookie trays for the employees, in my sleep in September and how effortlessly it went together. Everyone wanted to participate. The employees were so surprised and appreciative.

The miracle of this five-year-old, Maddy, sharing her hugs, her joy, her light with me in the morning.

The miracle of Blake dressed in her Halloween costume as a little old lady with her blow-up walker. Her joy, laughter, and light took my pain away for an entire day.

PRAYER FLAGS

As I have been writing this book, miracles keep happening. I was in my bedroom, and something (miracle) directed me to open a cabinet door in the bookcase Chuck designed. I found a plastic red twelve by twelve container. I had no idea what was in the container nor how it got there. I opened the container and found pictures of prayer flags from our fortieth wedding anniversary. I had not seen these pictures since 2007 and how they got into the bookcase is a mystery.

The story of the prayer flags.

The youngest nephew in our family, Ryan, was in college. He told my sister, Susan, and me that he was going to take some time off from school. He wanted to travel. Susan and I both said, "No you are not! Finish college, then you can travel." I remember when he finished college, he called me and said, "There I'm done! Now I get to travel."

He had a friend from Australia, so he went home with her to Australia. There he spent four months helping his friend on their ranch. After that he decided to travel to Europe. He backpacked across Europe for a while and then went to India and ended up in Tibet. He decided in Tibet to come back to Texas.

When he arrived in Houston, he called Susan, but she was out of town. She was coming in that day, so Ryan sat on the floor against a wall waiting for her plane to arrive. Susan had no idea that he was coming home. When she got off the plane, she noticed what she thought was a homeless person, sitting against the wall. As she walked by this person, this man said, "Mom!" Susan was stunned that it was Ryan. He had a full-grown beard, scruffy clothing and he was dirty all over. She took him home and got him all cleaned up.

Ryan brought a gift from Tibet for Chuck. He knew how much Chuck loved metaphysical teaching. Metaphysics is the study of reality and existence, who we are, and what is our purpose in this world.

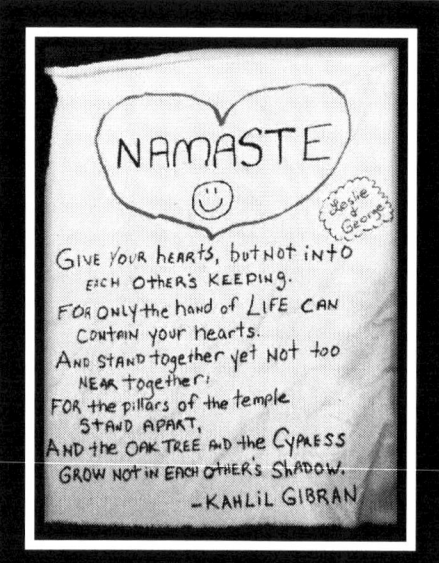
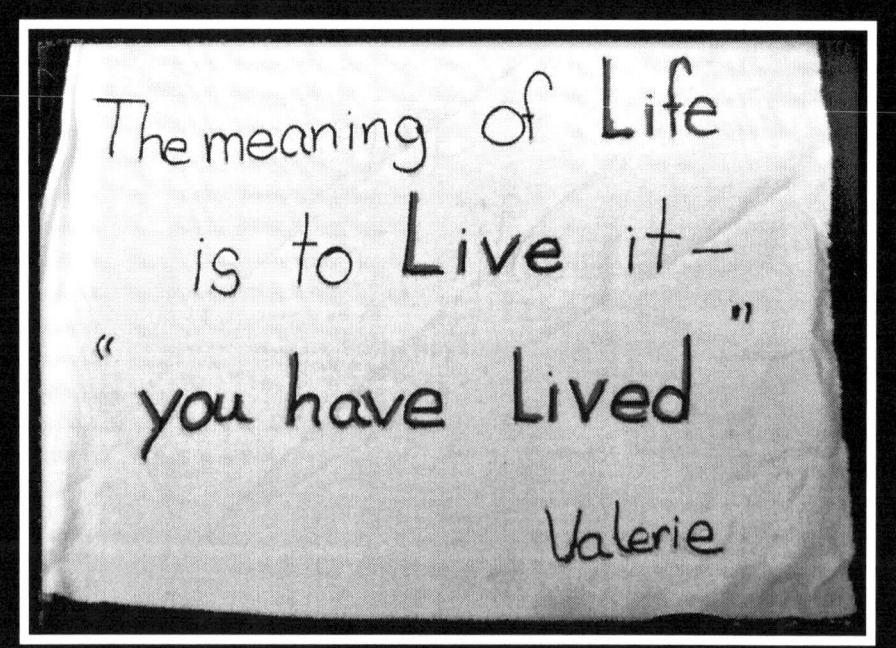

When Ryan was in Tibet, he purchased Tibetan Prayer Flags. Tibetan prayer flags are used to promote peace, compassion, strength, and wisdom. The flags do not carry prayers to gods, which is a common misconception; rather, the Tibetans believe the prayers and mantras will be blown by the wind to spread the good will and compassion into all-pervading space.

"Prayer flags fade with time and their color turns white. It is said that when the prayer flags turn white their prayers have been carried. When you decide to remove the prayer flags, don't just throw them away as it is considered disrespectful in Buddhist culture."

We had thirty-seven trees in our backyard, so Chuck and Ryan hung the flags from tree to tree. They did not turn white for quite a while.

Chuck and I were throwing a party for our fourth wedding anniversary. Friends and family were traveling from all over to attend the party. Valerie, friend/sister, cut up muslin fabric in an eight by twelve rectangle and sent a flag to each person coming to the party. Valerie came up early for the party and she presented to Chuck and me the prayer flags that everyone made. We were so surprised and thrilled to have this love from our family and friends. I took a picture of each flag before they got hung-up.

When everyone arrived, they looked in the trees and saw the flags. It was a beautiful sight. The flags lasted about three years before the messages were taken into the wind.

I found this tub just as I thought I had this book finished. God continues to show me the miracles in my life. Being able to revisit these pictures and what our family and friends wrote on the flags is a wonderful miracle and continued expression of love.

MIRACLES

Finding the red tub with the pictures of our prayer flags.

Ryan brought us the prayer flags from Tibet.

Valerie sending the flags to all our guests so they could write a message of love for us.

LESSONS FROM DENECE

Marriage Rules

There are four rules of marriage that I taught our girls:

One: Fall in love with your best friend. Their looks, height, and weight will not get you through the bad times and trust me, there will be bad times. Your best friend will get you through.

Two: Fall in love with 80 percent of that person. The other 20 percent you will never, ever change. Believe me, Chuck and I both tried.

Three: Understand, going into your marriage, that it is never ever 50-50. It is 90-10. When you think you are giving 90 and he/she is giving only 10 percent, they believe they are giving 90 and you are only giving 10 percent.

Four: If you are lucky, lust will last for one to two years. *Real* marriage is when you wake up in the morning, you have not combed your hair, you have not brushed your teeth, you have not shaved your arm pits or shaved your legs. He has not shaved his beard, brushed his teeth, put on deodorant, and he just farted — yet you still make love.

After I taught this to my girls, they both called me one day, a year or two into their marriages, and said, "Mom, you were so right!"

How to be an Advocate for your Loved One

Case Manager: A case manager assigns the administration of care for a patient with a serious or terminal illness to a single person (or team). This includes all necessary medical care, along with associated supportive services.

All insurance companies have what is called a "Case Manager." The role of the manager is to help *you* — the patient. They are the liaison between the insurance company, the doctor and *you*. Many times, a doctor will order a specific test or procedure and the insurance company will deny it. You the patient are caught in the middle. Your case manager steps in to get it approved by the insurance company.

Beverly was assigned a case manager early on in her journey. I did not realize that until I needed one. After the co-pay incident, I worked with her closely and she would even call periodically just to check in on how everything was going. She was extremely pivotal on the one occasion of Bev not paying her co-pay.

They are there for *you,* the patient, and your family.

End of Life Care

Five parts to a "No Code"

Being with Mother and Beverly as they died, taught me so much about the dying process. As I have written in both their stories, dying is a choice between God and your soul. You mentally don't get a vote and neither does anyone else.

As you age it is important to discuss with your family what your wishes are. How much do you want the medical community to do to keep you alive? Being part of the decision with your family will make your passing easier for everyone.

There are standards for a No Code, but you can design your own. It should be signed, dated, and witnessed by someone.

Many times, you will hear, "Oh, she's a No Code." So what does that mean?

There are five parts to a No Code. Everyone is told that there are four parts. But when Mother was in the Telemetry Unit, I discovered there are actually five parts.

A medical No Code is a directive you give to your doctor and your family. I have mine on file in my office and my girls have a copy. My medical team also has it in my records.

This directive tells everyone what my wishes are. It also alerts the hospital team to not perform emergency measures to sustain life. Be with me, please make me comfortable from pain, but do not stop the process from happening.

- No IV fluids: adding fluids to the body as the body is trying to shut down is very painful.

- No feeding tube: same as with fluids. Your organs are shutting down and it is painful for your body to try to process food.

- No Cardiac Pulmonary Resuscitation-CPR:_don't keep trying to keep my heart beating as it is trying to shut down.

- No Resuscitation: don't put me on a machine to keep my lungs breathing. Once you are on a ventilator, it is emotionally hard to pull that plug.

- Chemical No Code: when Mother was on the telemetry unit, her body was shooting small blood clots. Slowly she lost the ability to speak. She could only do one- syllable words. The doctor gave her a medication for her body to stop shooting TIAs (transient ischemic attack) — a short period of symptoms like those of a stroke. It is caused by a brief blockage of blood flow to the brain.

GODSENDS IN MY LIFE

Although I could not find a Google definition for it, I believe there are "Godsends" in our lives. My definition of a Godsend is someone God sends to you at a time in your life when you really need help or support. Sometimes they stay in your life forever. Sometimes they come in for a specific time in your life, then go away.

Barbara Ferguson Gillium. I met Barbara in seventh grade. We became fast friends and have stayed friends to this day. Barbara introduced me to Rainbow Girls, which became my first connection with God. It taught me self-respect, leadership, and giving to others. All lessons that have carried me through my entire life. Barbara was a bridesmaid at my wedding and helped Chuck and I celebrate our 50th wedding anniversary.

In August of 2017, Barbara came up from Texas to help us celebrate our golden wedding anniversary. In October of that year, I was having a knee replacement on my right knee. Barb handed me a prayer she had written. It helped me so much as I was going into surgery. When I was in rehab for four weeks, I had the prayer right by my side. Today this prayer is taped to the wall in my study, to guide me throughout my day.

I AM NOT AFRAID, BECAUSE…

I am blessed by the knee appliance that has served me so well for so many years.

I am blessed by the new appliance that will fit perfectly and serve me the rest of my years on earth.

I am blessed by the Lord who guides me and gives me the strength to handle all challenges.

I am blessed by my loving husband and cherished daughters who light up my life every day.

I am blessed by my precious granddaughters who bring immense joy and pride to my world.

I am blessed by the surgeon and his team who will use their God-given talents and skills to restore my health and mobility.

I am blessed by my home team of loving friends and my precious sister.

I know I will emerge from the challenge, recovered and restored, and *believe it*. I thank the universe now, in advance, and forever.

I close my eyes and see myself completely recovered and restored and *believe it*. I thank the universe now, in advance, and forever.

I know I will emerge as a blessed woman capable of giving *blessings* to others.

I accept that I am not in charge, but I am being guided and directed by you, Lord, and your way is perfect.

I am not afraid for I am immensely blessed.

Mr. Sweeney, my speech teacher from Alamo Heights High School in San Antonio, Texas. He was my teacher for speech and drama my junior and senior year. He taught me to enunciate, to not say "Git" but "Get," to not say "Jest" but "Just", to not say "Gunna" but "Going to."

The lessons he taught me have carried me throughout my life. I was able to tell him what he had done for me at my 40th high school reunion. He was with his wife when I went up to him.

He stood up as I took both of his hands and said, "Mr. Sweeney, you are not going to remember me because I was not one of your stellar students. But I have been waiting to tell you this for 40 years. When I spoke at the national Longaberger Basket Convention, *you* were on my shoulder, helping me to enunciate and speak correctly. When I ran for school board for the Valley View School district, *you* were on my shoulder. As I would give speeches and presentations for Valley View, *you* were always on my shoulders. You, Mr. Sweeney, *you* are my Mr. Holland's Opus, the teacher who made a huge influence on my life."

Kirke and Janene Jefferies arranged a blind date for Chuck and me. That date was when I met my soulmate. They set up the blind date as a joke because we were such opposites. Chuck was an introvert, and I am an extrovert.

Police officer in Houston. Right after Chuck and I were married, we moved to Houston. When we were interviewing for jobs, I was in downtown Houston waiting for Chuck to pick me up. The police officer was my God-send that took care of me and kept me safe.

Doctor at the mental institute. He took away my extra guilt about my dad when telling me we had done "the right thing" for Dad.

Valerie Flynn. I met Val when I was president of the PTA at Valley View. We were greeting the new kindergarten students. Valerie brought her youngest child, Jean, into the school to learn about the kindergarten program.

Valerie and I hit it off right away. We are both seamstresses. She has been by my side through every major event in my life. She has been there to take care of me through every surgery. In 2001, when I was having my first knee replacement, I asked her to come up for three months to help me heal and take me to physical therapy.

At first, Chuck said, "Val is coming for three months?" Then after the first day she was with us, he said, "That is the smartest decision you have ever made." Val's being there would allow Chuck to go back to work and not worry about me.

When Chuck died in 2020, Val gave up five months of her life to be with me. I know I would not have made it without her. Valerie has become my sister.

Diana Yost. Diana is a licensed professional counselor. When I was going through the four huge losses in my life, Diana was the person that made me whole again. I counseled with her for four years, weekly, to put me back together. She is still a part of my life.

When Chuck announced he was retiring from his job at Thomas Associates, I told him six months before he retired, "We are going to Diana for counseling. This is a monumental change for you and a huge change for me. You may have paid for this house, but I own this house. I have been a stay-at-home spouse for most of our marriage, and you are now entering my world."

Diana has helped and guided me through every major event in my life. When Chuck died in 2020, she helped me deal with this devasting loss in my life.

I asked Diana to write the Foreword to my book.

Bonnie Wilson. Bonnie and I met through a club called New Westsider's. It was a club for new people moving to the west side of Cleveland. Bonnie introduced me to P.E.O., an organization I strongly believe in and one that will be with me forever. It is truly a gift.

Lucinda Kessinger. Lucinda came into my life after Chuck died. She worked in my house packing me up and getting rid of stuff. Lucinda came in every day, collaborated with me for five hours, then came back the next day. She was always pleasant, and our friendship grew. We would go to a room in the house, and she would tag what I wanted to keep or put tags on what the family wanted. Then she would go to work packing my stuff to take with me. She put the boxes in the POD parked on my driveway. She had her workspace set up in the living room. I could not have packed all the things I wanted and made my move to Minnesota without Lucinda.

Mari Chorn. I met Mari at my new home in Minnesota, Riley Crossing. Mari fell in love with Sydney. Mari is 87 and came to see Sydney every day. In the spring, summer, and fall, she would take Sydney for a short walk around the building. Sydney adored her. I was concerned about Sydney and how she would adjust. She had lost her Chuck, moved from her home, and gave up her huge backyard in Westlake. Because of Mari, Sydney adjusted fine.

Kelly Neff. Kelly and Leslie graduated high school in the same class. Kelly was also in my Brownie Troop in elementary school.

Four years ago, Kelly lost her husband, Randy. She has put significant effort into healing and reinventing her purpose in life. She started her career in coaching, so Kelly and I started working together a year ago. She has become a life coach, and I was one of her first clients. She has helped me to value my talents.

In my sewing, I never did alterations before. I wanted to make things from scratch, not repair broken things. In the beginning as I worked on alterations, I did not value my sewing talents. With Kelly's help, I now value my sewing abilities. With the money I have made doing alterations, I bought a new iPad and paid *cash* for it instead of charging it. I felt enormously proud of myself. Now I am saving for a cruise for February of 2024.

Jan Davis. While Chuck was with me, I had confidence that he would walk me through the chronic pain episodes. My pain doctor from The Cleveland Clinic developed a pain cream that rubs on whatever area that has flared up.

When I moved to Minnesota, I wondered how I was going to put this cream on. At Riley Crossing, I met my next-door neighbor, Jan Davis. Jan is so wonderful. I can call her anytime and she will rub the cream on me. She is truly a Godsend.

I have been so blessed that God has sent these people to me throughout my life.
When you think of your life, can you find the Godsends?

HOW I CHOOSE TO LIVE MY LIFE

This Declaration hangs in front of me at my desk. This is how I choose to live my life every day:

I want to lead my life in total flow and joy, never struggling.
I expect miracles to happen.
It comes because I am beginning to see that I don't manifest everything in my life. God does.
I have permission to slow down, turn this to God, and watch it happen.
I will experience twice the joy at half the speed and twice the business.
Ask if the speed that I move in is the speed that God wants me to move in. Is there any direction that God wants me to move in.
There is truth in opening the possibilities of slowing down and receiving more.

Dream True

When my girls were growing up and they lost something, I taught them about "Dreaming True." I have always believed nothing is ever lost. If I lost something, I would pray and turn it over to God, then let go. If it was meant for me to have it, it would show up again.

Many times, I have dreamed about where it is or saw where it was in my dreams. If it did not show up, then it was not meant for me. Maybe it was for someone else.

This happened with Chuck's Merkabah and my cross necklace.

Another Prayer

This prayer is also in front of me in my office:

Good morning, this is God.

Today, I will be handling all of your problems. Please remember that I do not need your help. If the devil happens to deliver a situation to you that you cannot handle, do not attempt to resolve it. Kindly put it in the SFGTD (Something for God to Do) box. It will be addressed in my time, not yours.

Once the matter is placed into the box, do not hold onto it nor remove it. Holding on or removal will delay the resolution of your problem. If it is a situation you think you are capable of handling, please consult me in prayer to be sure that it is the proper resolution. Because I do not sleep, nor do I slumber, there is no need for you to lose any sleep. Please rest my child.

If you need to contact me, I am only a prayer away. My prayer line is open 24 hours of your day. I love you and will always be with you wherever you may go. As with all good things, pass my message on.

Love, GOD

Prayer inspired by Second Corinthians 5:7
Anonymous Author

"Father God, open my eyes, not to see the world more clearly, but to see You. Open my eyes to see You working around me and in me. Nothing happens by accident. You orchestrate every day of my life. Allow me to see Your hand in the mundane and the fantastic. Help me to trust in what I cannot see and believe in Your invisible presence."

Final Thought:

GOD is nearer than your next breath. That in itself is a miracle. Think about it…the creator of all things is nearer to YOU than your next breath!

ACKNOWLEDGEMENTS

I want to thank our Lord for telling me for seven years that I was going to write a book on the miracles in my life. I kept saying, "I can't write a book!" He never let go of me drafting this book.

I also want to thank my wonderful husband, **Chuck**. From day one of our meeting each other, he always believed in me. He encouraged me to listen to God about writing this book. He would be so proud of me. I also want to thank my family. My girls and their husbands have always believed I could do this.

I want to thank **Dr. Stuart Ervay**, my brother-in-law. Stu has authored many books. He was a professor at Emporia State University. He had been married for years to my husband's sister, Barbara. Barbara developed Alzheimer's and Stu has written a book on taking care of an Alzheimer's wife from a man's perspective. This book is entitled *Confronting Dementia: A Husband's Journey as an Alzheimer's Caregiver* and is available on Amazon.

I want to thank four friends at Riley Crossing who encouraged me to write my book:

Elsie Fuhrman (*Baptized in the Holy Spirit*), "This book was written to inform believers what it means to be baptized in the Holy Spirit. My husband and I taught classes on this subject for many years. Throughout the years we have encountered many comments and questions about this experience of the Holy Spirit. This book is an attempt to provide some explanations and answers. Because there are many misconceptions about the experience of being baptized in the Holy Spirit, we felt there was a need for material that would be helpful to the body of Christ in understanding this encounter with the Holy Spirit."

Linda Herman (*In and Out of the Clouds*), "Best views from my office window. For many years I kept a journal about my flying experiences. Exciting trips with great layovers, locally and around the world, meeting wonderful people along the way and working with dedicated (as I was) co-workers. I'm hoping my next book will be bigger than my first tiny one. I have a lot more stories I would like to share with everyone. Hope you can place yourself on my jump seat. Enjoy the view and the ride. I wanted those reading the book and seeing my photos to feel like they were right there with me on every leg of my journey. You can purchase my little book by going to Amazon.com Linda Sue.

Bill Shogren (*What is it about Eau Claire?*), "The first book I wrote was because I was experienced in fly fishing for trout. I co-authored a book on the subject. Some call it the Bible for trout anglers. That felt good. The third writers' group I joined was much better because of meeting Elna. Elna encouraged me to put my stories into book form. I thought about it but didn't act on it. In this third group I met Char Howard. The group met at her home. Again, many people had written very serious stories. When I read my stories, they laughed and loved my stories about my childhood. I gave them comic relief. They said I should publish a book. I did, *What it is About Eau Claire?* I must say, Elna was the biggest influence on me."

Bonnie Smith Bobbie is a retired English teacher and agreed to be my beta reader for my book. She would correct the spelling and punctuation. I had never met anyone who had written a book until I moved to Riley Crossing and met three authors who have written books. Meeting them made me say I was going to give this book writing a chance.

ABOUT THE AUTHOR

Denece Black Praeger was born in San Antonio, Texas, and spent her childhood there. She was raised in a military family and had two sisters. She has one year of college. During her freshman year of college, at eighteen, she met Chuck Praeger. They dated for one year and got married in 1967. They have two daughters, Leslie and Laura. She also has two grandchildren.

When Chuck and Denece married, they both decided that she would be a stay-at-home mom and raise their girls. She was very active in their lives from Scout leader, PTA, to volunteering at school. When the girls graduated from school, she became active in politics and was president of the Valley View Board of Education in Germantown, Ohio. While serving, Denece helped revamp the high school leadership.

When she got married, her mother bought her a sewing machine and said, "Learn to make your own clothes and your children's clothes." Denece discovered she loved sewing and took every sewing class she could find to become an expert seamstress, making everything from her own underwear to her husband's suits, upholstery, and drapes.

Denece was an award-winning consultant for The Longaberger Company and ran a successful business out-of-her-home, managing 57 consultants nationwide. She also started a cake business out of her home, making wedding cakes and special occasion cakes, developing her own cake recipe for the cakes. She ran this business for 12 years.

When her sister, Beverly, developed breast cancer, Denece started a luncheon in her family room, to support research for breast cancer. This grew from her family room to becoming a 501c3 organization, "Journey of Hope."

As Denece has entered her senior years, she lives at Riley Crossing Senior Living Facility in Chanhassen, MN. There she is active in the social activities for the residents.

One of the main focuses for Denece is to live her life doing God's work. As she started recognizing that miracles were happening in her life, she decided to write her book to help others realize that miracles are happening in their lives every day as well.

Follow Denece on Facebook and leave reviews of *Miracles in My Life* on Amazon.

Made in the USA
Middletown, DE
06 February 2025

70187404R00084